Frank Ormsby was born in Enniskillen in 1947 and was educated there at St Michael's College and later at Queen's University Belfast. He is head of English at the Royal Belfast Academical Institution. In 1974 he won an Eric Gregory Award for his poetry, and his two collections, *A Store of Candles* (Oxford University Press, 1977; Gallery Press, 1986) and *A Northern Spring* (Secker and Warburg/Gallery Press, 1986), were both Poetry Book Society choices. He edited the first edition of *Poets from the North of Ireland* (1979), *Northern Windows: An Anthology of Ulster Autobiography* (1987) and *The Long Embrace: Twentieth-century Irish Love Poems* (1987), all published by Blackstaff Press. He was an editor of the *Honest Ulsterman* from 1969 to 1989.

POETS

from the

NORTH

of

IRELAND

New Edition

edited by

Frank
Ormsby

THE
BLACKSTAFF PRESS
BELFAST

ACKNOWLEDGEMENT

The editor gratefully acknowledges the financial help
of The Arts Council of Northern Ireland.

First edition published in 1979 by
The Blackstaff Press Limited

This fully revised and updated edition published in 1990 by
The Blackstaff Press Limited
3 Galway Park, Dundonald, Belfast BT16 0AN, Northern Ireland
with the assistance of
The Arts Council of Northern Ireland

© Selection, Introduction and Notes, Frank Ormsby, 1979, 1990
All rights reserved
The acknowledgements on pp. 325–9 constitute an extension
of this copyright page

Typeset by Textflow Services Limited

Printed by The Guernsey Press Company Limited

British Library Cataloguing in Publication Data

Poetry from the North of Ireland. –Full rev. and updated ed.
1. Poetry in English. Northern Irish writers, 1900–
I. Ormsby, Frank 1947–
821.9120809416
ISBN 0-85640-444-6

CONTENTS

Poets from the North of Ireland has been in print for over ten years and an enlarged, updated edition reflecting the transitions and developments of the 1980s has now become necessary. The two elder poets to whom the anthology was originally dedicated, John Hewitt and George Buchanan, both died during the decade. For them and many other poets represented in the first edition, the 1980s were a period of consolidation. Hewitt, in particular, enjoyed more attention and homage in his final years than for most of his creative life and his status was further recognised in the founding of the John Hewitt International Summer School in 1988, a year after his death. *The Selected John Hewitt* appeared in 1980 and there were 'selected' editions of the work of a number of other poets: Padraic Fiacc, Roy McFadden, Robert Greacen, John Montague, James Simmons, Seamus Heaney, Seamus Deane and Paul Muldoon. Michael Longley and Derek Mahon published what were virtually 'collected' volumes, though both have continued to produce new books. A fresh selection of Louis MacNeice's work, edited by Michael Longley, also appeared, one of many indications of MacNeice's growing reputation and influence on northern poetry. Most of those represented in the original edition of this anthology have produced substantial books of poems since 1980 and a number of gifted poets have emerged in recent years, one of whom, Medbh McGuckian, has already established herself as a powerful, innovative force in Irish poetry. The poetic activity of the decade was complemented by the appearance of Hewitt's selected prose, MacNeice's selected criticism and prose, Montague's selected essays, two volumes of prose by Seamus Heaney and a selection of essays by Tom Paulin. The amount of critical commentary on northern poetry has also increased considerably and I have tried to reflect this in the bibliographical notes on individual poets and in the Select Bibliography.

This edition contains selections from twenty-seven northern poets born since 1900, each of whom has published at least one book-length collection. It does not aim to be exhaustively representative. A list of absent qualifiers would include John Lyle Donaghy, John Irvine, Maurice James Craig, Geoffrey Squires, Francis Harvey, Shaun Traynor, Michael Brophy, Catherine Bryon, Dennis Greig and Tom Morgan. A case could be made for the inclusion of Patrick Kavanagh (County Monaghan), Tom MacIntyre (County Cavan), Matthew Sweeney and D.J. O'Sullivan (County Donegal), as well as George McWhirter (born in Belfast and living in Canada, where his books are published) and Alan Alexander (from Strabane, County Tyrone, who lives and is published in Australia). Of the northern women poets born since 1900 – Barbara Hunter, Freda Laughton, Meta Mayne Reid, Eleanor Murray and Joan Newmann, for example – few have published in book form. There is, too, a body of work in Irish by poets from Northern Ireland, much of it as yet untranslated; and a number of English poets have lived in the north and written out of their experience there: Philip Larkin, Norman Dugdale, Philip Hobsbaum, Andrew Waterman, Wes Magee and Paul Wilkins come to mind. The anthologies listed in the Select Bibliography will, perhaps, help to complete the picture.

I hope that this edition will, like its predecessor, introduce general readers to northern poetry of the present and the immediate past and that it will gain for the younger poets in particular a wider audience than they could otherwise expect at the beginning of their writing careers.

Finally, an expression of regret and an expression of gratitude. The publisher Faber and Faber declined to allow the inclusion of more than twelve poems each by Louis MacNeice and Paul Muldoon; I deeply regret that this compelled me, in the interest of maintaining at least a semblance of 'balance', to restructure the anthology at a late date, reducing the representation not only of these two poets but of a number of others not published by Faber and Faber. I am grateful to the poets affected and their publishers, who have, without exception, been understanding and supportive.

INTRODUCTION

Written poetry began in the north of Ireland, as elsewhere in the country, with the work of the bardic poet or *ollamh*. His patrons were the Gaelic chieftains of clans such as the O'Neills, the O'Donnells and the Maguires, for whom he composed eulogies in return for reward and protection and about whom, in other circumstances, he might write satires. His status was complex: in a country that had adopted Christianity without entirely relinquishing paganism, he was semi-druidic, his social position roughly equivalent to that of a Christian bishop. The power of the *ollamh* declined after the defeat of the native Irish at the Battle of Kinsale in 1602 and the Flight of the Earls in 1607, but Gaelic poetry survived in the monasteries and elsewhere until the late eighteenth century. Its last notable flowering occurred in counties Cavan, Louth and Meath, and in south Armagh, in the work of such poets as Séamus Dall Mac Cuarta, Cathal Buí Mac Giolla Gunna, Peadar Ó Doirnín and Art Mac Cubthaigh.

Following the Flight of the Earls, the north was colonised by English and Scottish settlers and the descendants of these groups began to emerge in discernible literary movements at roughly the same time as the Gaelic tradition was fading. The peasant weaver, farmer, and schoolmaster poets of south and mid-Antrim and north and north-east Down, who flourished at the end of the eighteenth century and in the first half of the nineteenth, had as their literary language a version of Lowlands Scots, and as their poetic exemplars, Scottish poets such as Robert Sempill, Sir David Lindsay, Alexander Montgomerie, Allan Ramsay and, of course, Robert Burns. It is appropriate that the peasant poets' names are associated with particular places – James Orr of Ballycarry, Hugh Porter of Moneyslan, James Campbell of Ballynure – for not only did their verse reflect the work, character, customs and everyday existence of the people among whom they lived, but these people gave them patronage in the form of subscriptions to their books. With the movement of the linen industry into mills and factories, this upsurge of peasant poets lost its impetus and poetry in English

1

became the preserve of educated men of Planter background who looked to England for their literary models, though their subjects were sometimes Irish. One such group, associated with Bishop Thomas Percy at Dromore, County Down, had flourished concurrently with the peasant poets already mentioned, but Percy died in 1811 and the best poets outside the Dromore group, Dr William Drennan and James Stuart, died in 1820 and 1848 respectively. Northern poetry may be said to have survived the century in the work of northerners living elsewhere: Sir Samuel Ferguson (1810–86) and Thomas Caulfield Irwin (1823–92) in Dublin, and William Allingham (1824–89) in London.

Ferguson's poetry is significantly transitional. He was descended from Scottish planters, but was so immersed in the native Irish tradition that his work is more nationalistic than colonial. In fact his English imitations of bardic poems make him an acknowledged precursor of W.B. Yeats and the Irish Literary Renaissance, a movement by which the poets associated with the Ulster Literary Theatre in the early years of the twentieth century were in turn heavily influenced. George Russell (AE) left the north to become one of the pillars of the renaissance and the work of Alice Milligan, Joseph Campbell and James H. Cousins, for example, reflects the concerns of the Celtic Twilight writers as faithfully as that of the poets based in Dublin. By the early 1920s most of the Ulster Literary Theatre poets had left the north or ceased to publish. The period from 1920 to 1930 was a comparatively lean one, most memorable, perhaps, for the dramatic monologues of the linen magnate Richard Rowley, in which he attempts to give dialect voice to Belfast's factory workers, and for the vigorous 'folk' poetry of the County Tyrone brothers, W.F. Marshall and R.L. Marshall.

One could list the decades during which the poets represented in this anthology began to acquire reputations, but to do so would give little sense of the continuity of northern poetry. John Hewitt and George Buchanan, for example, wrote poems in the 1920s, but did not appear in book form until 1948 and 1958 respectively, and published their final collections in the 1980s, Buchanan in 1982 and Hewitt in 1986. Indeed most of the poets in these pages have published book-length collections in the 1980s, the exceptions being Louis MacNeice, W.R. Rodgers and Tom Matthews.

What follows is an introductory survey, not a critical study. I hope it will give the reader some sense of what the twenty-seven poets in the anthology have in common and how they differ from one another.

1

When George Buchanan's collection *Bodily Responses* appeared in 1958 he was fifty-four years old and had already published two journals, five novels and a volume of autobiography. *Bodily Responses* and subsequent collections are the work of one who has found his way gradually towards a particular subject matter and style through the discovery of his central themes in the journals and novels and in the sometimes 'poetic' quality of his prose.

The titles of four of his collections – *Bodily Responses, Conversation with Strangers, Minute-Book of a City* and *Possible Being* – are pointers to Buchanan's pervasive concerns. His poems may be regarded as salvoes in a campaign against what he calls (in the Preface to *Bodily Responses*) 'aesthetic and emotional impoverishment'. He advocates an intense, receptive awareness of the present, a willingness for people to immerse themselves intelligently and feelingly in the life of twentieth-century cities. For him the artist is a spiritual revolutionary, an anticipator who posits a society in which sensitivity and open-mindedness will replace institutionalised responses, apathy and indifference. He distrusts systems and hierarchies and those who are contemptuous of the masses, he rejects aggression and materialism, and prefers an embracing of the 'not-yet-there' to nostalgia. He asks, as in 'War-and-peace', that life be lived as a dynamic synthesis, a controlled collision with the environment and the instant. Underlying all these concerns is a vision of human beings as 'world members' and, coupled with his vulnerable belief in this, a determination (like that he attributes to Lewis Mumford) to outstare the cynics.

Buchanan was of Planter descent and grew up in rural Antrim

3

but neither circumstance is central to his poetry. The first considerable laureate of these areas of northern experience is John Hewitt. In the Foreword to his *Collected Poems 1932–1967* (1968) he defines himself as 'by birth an Irishman of Planter stock, by profession an art gallery man, politically a man of the Left', and insisted on the relevance of these facts 'in the conditioning of [his] response to experience'. Six years later, in an *Irish Times* symposium on 'The clash of identities' (4 July 1974) he states his 'hierarchy of values' in the following terms:

> I'm an Ulsterman of Planter stock. I was born in the island of Ireland, so secondly I'm an Irishman. I was born in the British archipelago and English is my native tongue, so I am British. The British archipelago are offshore islands to the continent of Europe, so I'm European.

This lucid statement strongly suggests a man who has thought out his opinion, who knows where he stands, and to a certain extent this is true of Hewitt: but it is at the point where those certainties end that the tensions of his poetry begin. To be native to a province colonised by ancestors, at home and yet 'alien', a city man who loves, but must struggle to relate to, the country, someone aware (as in 'O country people') of gaps that are finally unbridgeable, is to be perpetually unsure of one's place. Ultimately, Hewitt's poetry is a restlessly contemplative, universal quest for self-definition, personally and in relation to society, environment and history.

Louis MacNeice was, like Hewitt, conscious of the factors in his background and upbringing that cut him off from the 'candles of the Irish poor' and was, too, caught in endless cycles of fascination and repulsion in his attitudes to Ireland. Poems about Ireland represent a small fraction of his output and he spent most of his school, university and professional life in England; nevertheless his work is permeated by the experiences of his childhood years in Carrickfergus, County Antrim. Listing influences, he includes 'having been brought up in the north of Ireland, having a father who was a clergyman, the fact that my mother died when I was little'. He also mentions early contacts with mental illness (his mother's) and mental abnormality (he had a brother who suffered from Down's syndrome) and the fact that the house in Carrickfergus was lit by oil lamps and was therefore shadowy, as contributing to the imagery of petrification, fear, anxiety, loneliness and monotony so prevalent in his poetry. They may also, he adds, explain 'an excessive preoccupation in my earlier work with things dazzling, high-coloured, quick-moving, hedonistic or up-to-date'.

It is not only in his earlier work that MacNeice is preoccupied with the 'up-to-date'. All his poetic life he was fascinated both by the trivia and the most serious issues of the time. This is especially obvious in the poems he wrote in the 1930s, when he was considered one of the leading poets of his generation. The central concerns of 1930s literature are present in his work: economic decline, unemployment, the rise of fascism, the Spanish Civil War, the imminence and outbreak of World War II. The ominous and disturbing elements in MacNeice's poetry are partly balanced by his joyful recognition of the vigorous plurality of existence, its endless, bright assault on the senses, and of the triumphant or forlorn power of love in the face of menace, whether from war or time.

Buchanan and MacNeice were the sons of clergymen and their scepticism and vitality of response to the world are, partly at least, reactions against their backgrounds. The same may be said of the poetry of W.R. Rodgers, who was himself a Presbyterian minister for eleven years before leaving the Church to join the BBC. He published only two collections of poems in his lifetime, but his sensuous celebration of the world and the sheer exuberance of his language gave his output a meteoric intensity.

In a radio talk entitled 'On writing a poem', Rodgers described words as being 'like county councillors: they have always hosts of relations who are looking for employment', and as a poet he was an enthusiastic patron of the linguistic unemployed. Words were his best friends and worst enemies; he could exploit their inherent nepotism to give a startling, highly imaginative, highly infectious picture of, say, a swan or a windy day, but was too often tempted away from his thematic centre into the mere froth of linguistic performance. He is at his most powerful when writing on religious or biblical themes with a

5

restrained freshness of language, as in 'Lent' and 'The net', where technical expertise is harnessed and concentrated, or in 'Resurrection: an Easter sequence', where the diction is comparatively plain, the form loose and the freshness partly in the use of contemporary colloquialism, partly in the 'humanising' effect of this on the characters involved. His best descriptive poetry has what Matthew Arnold referred to as 'the power of so dealing with things as to awaken in us a wonderfully full, new, and intimate sense of them, and of our relations with them', and his best religious verse enacts convincingly a drama of joy and austerity, of puritan values and sensuous affirmation of the world and the flesh, of human and divine.

Among the other poets who emerged in the early 1940s were Robert Greacen and Roy McFadden, both of whom reacted against what they regarded as backward-looking and provincial in Irish poetry and were influenced for a time by the New Apocalypse or New Romantic movement in England. Greacen's early collections, *One Recent Evening* (1944) and *The Undying Day* (1948), are heavily derivative of this movement in mood, imagery and diction and only occasionally does he begin to find an individual voice. Almost thirty years elapsed before the appearance of his third collection, the serio-comic *A Garland for Captain Fox* (1975), in which he creates a suave, mysterious con man who is both absurd and dangerous. Greacen has written on a wide variety of subjects but his most memorable poems are a series of elegies, ranging from the ominous, much-anthologised wartime poem 'The bird' to the more light-hearted summoning of family ghosts in 'Carnival at the river'.

The elegiac note is more morbidly predominant in the early collections of Greacen's friend Roy McFadden, a writer burdened from the beginning with a pacifist's awareness of the nightmare of history. However, McFadden's third book, *The Heart's Townland* (1947), in which he expresses some disagreement with the stance and outlook of John Hewitt, shows him beginning to develop, stylistically and thematically, along lines pioneered by the older poet. *The Garryowen* (1971) and its successor, *Verifications* (1977), represent a further development as McFadden belatedly discovers subject areas from which he was originally diverted. There is a process of salvage, rediscovery, re-evaluation, and though the poems are sometimes loosely nostalgic, the most memorable show an intense imaginative power, particularly the sequence 'Contemplations of Mary'. Some of McFadden's most recent work draws on his experience as a solicitor and presents an absorbing mixture of professional observation and personal involvement. *A Watching Brief* (1979), *Letters to the Hinterland* (1986) and *After Seymour's Funeral* (1990) offer a perspective on the past that is by turns morose, pained, sardonic, cautiously affirmative.

By the Black Stream, Odour of Blood, Nights in the Bad Place, Missa Terribilis – Padraic Fiacc's titles are as indicative as George Buchanan's of the tone and content of the collections they name. Storm, illness, death, the hardness of industrial Belfast, the violence of Irish history and its shadow over the present, are Fiacc's obsessive themes and his vision has become increasingly dark. His poems have an agonised directness in their treatment of personal and political turmoil and are peopled largely by victims and casualties. He is at his most effective in the controlled, melancholic cadences of, for example, 'Gloss' and 'Intimate letter 1973', or when his work is given depth by religious and other myths. His reaction to the violence of Northern Ireland is sometimes strident and hysterical, but his characteristic voice, harrowingly intense, mordantly humorous, is entirely his own.

John Montague, like Fiacc, was born in New York of Irish immigrant parents, but was raised on his aunts' farm in County Tyrone. Introducing his long poem *The Rough Field* in 1972, he wrote that he sometimes saw it 'as taking over where the last bard of the O'Neills left off', and of all the poets of comparable origin represented here, he is the one most conscious of himself as the inheritor of a 'lost tradition' and of the historical events that force him to express his awareness in a 'grafted tongue'. Influenced, perhaps, by Patrick Kavanagh's poems about County Monaghan, he was also the first twentieth-century poet from north of the border to write in depth about the rural community in which he grew up; in this respect he is himself a major influence on a number of younger northern poets. Montague identifies with the people whose lives he depicts, but is also

7

sufficiently distanced from them by education to see them not only as individuals but also as representatives of a dying culture. In particular, his old women are, on one level, related to the personifications of Ireland common in Gaelic literature. He is both elegist and celebrator. The tone of his rural and historical poems is primarily, but not wholly, one of lament; he is clear-sightedly aware of what was barbaric or limiting in the tradition he mourns, but he knows even more keenly what vitality and indigenous strength have been lost. The elegiac and celebratory notes are struck again in his love poetry. His earliest collections show an awareness of what is emotionally crippling in Irish attitudes to love and sex; his own love lyrics, painfully honest, tenderly sensual, are among the most moving in Irish poetry.

2

The 1960s were a springboard period for poetry in the north of Ireland. One possible reason for this was an increase in the number of educated Catholics, a consequence of the Education Act of 1947. More immediately, the writers' group formed by the English poet Philip Hobsbaum, who was then lecturing at Queen's University Belfast, provided a regular opportunity for emerging poets – Seamus Heaney, Michael Longley and James Simmons among them – to read their work to a critical audience. The group continued to meet for some years after Hobsbaum's departure. In 1965 Michael Emmerson, the director of the Queen's University Festival (later the Belfast Festival at Queen's), pro-moted a series of Festival Publications which included the first pamphlet collections of Heaney, Longley, Simmons, Derek Mahon and Seamus Deane. Harry Chambers's magazine *Phoe-nix* (1965–75), the first few issues of which appeared from Belfast, was another significant platform; and in 1968 James Simmons founded the *Honest Ulsterman* magazine, which be-came an outlet for the poets already mentioned and for genera-tions of their successors. The Arts Council of Northern Ireland responded by granting subsidies to various publications and by promoting reading tours: the first was *Room to Rhyme* (1968), with Heaney, Longley and the folk singer David Hammond, and it

8

was followed in the 1970s by *The Planter and the Gael* (1970–71), with Hewitt and Montague, *Out of the Blue* (1974), with Simmons and Paul Muldoon, and *In their Element* (1977), with Heaney and Mahon.

James Simmons's stance is that of the reformer or secular evangelist who is firmly on the side of life and freedom, but who possesses an ironic self-awareness. The drama of his poetry often lies in the pitting of theory against personal experience and human fallibility, especially in relation to love, sex, marriage, the family, growing old. Not only is he engaged in exploring the quicksands of passion, joy, possessiveness, jealousy, betrayal, emotional dishonesty, unhappiness, but also in a campaign against the élitist image and minority attraction of poetry. Simmons is a writer and singer of songs as well as a poet and his poetry constantly aspires to the accessibility and popular appeal of song. He does not always avoid the dangers of oversimplicity, indulgent confessionalism and flatness of style which are inherent in his approach, but his best poems have a startling directness that clarifies the complexity of life without diminishing it, a note of sympathy and celebration, a convincing sense of how people can, to adapt his own words, muddle through to ecstasy or revelation. The quotidian and the apparently banal are the material of Simmons's poetry, but because he sees life and literature as inseparably linked, he can make fertile use of characters from, for example, *King Lear* and *The Tempest*, as a means of self-analysis, or use art as an illuminating perspective on reality, and vice versa. Collections such as *Constantly Singing* (1980), and *From the Irish* (1985) – which includes vigorous adaptions of well-known Gaelic poems – show his continuing preoccupation with 'natural forces, marriages, divorces', as well as reaffirming his relish for the grace and courage of those who face life smiling and for the painfully comforting fact that 'problems keep pushing us towards solutions'. Simmons's refusal to be disenchanted is among his most engaging qualities.

A consolidating factor in the poetic activity of the 1960s was the immediate success of Seamus Heaney's first collection, *Death of a Naturalist* (1966). The book establishes Heaney as the new explorer of territories charted by Patrick Kavanagh and John

Montague. His education has isolated him from his rural background, but he is constantly aware of his poetry as a craft akin to the traditional crafts of turf-cutter, ploughman, thatcher, water-diviner, salmon-fisher, mummer and blacksmith. *Death of a Naturalist* also establishes Heaney's characteristic use of rich, muscular language to convey the sights, sounds and texture of the countryside, the awareness in his poetry of digging as a metaphor for personal and historical excavation and his interest in bogland, which he comes to see in later poems as a bottomless repository of the past. Heaney's reading of the Danish archaeologist P.V. Glob's book *The Bog People*, an account of the sacrificial victims of fertility rites in Iron Age Scandinavia, led him, in his collections *Wintering Out* (1972) and *North* (1975), to attempt an illumination of Irish, and especially recent Northern Irish, history in terms of tribal mores, though in *North* he also approaches the subject through his own experience. In the collections which follow, Heaney continues to look north to the sources of his inspiration, but also outwards to European literature (to Dante's *Divine Comedy*, for example, and the work of twentieth-century Eastern European poets) for imaginative stimulus and sustenance. He quarrels with himself about his responsibilities as a poet, feeling a deep obligation to write about events in Northern Ireland and a yearning to be free of that pressure; he explores marriage and fatherhood and mourns the dead in lyrics of profound emotional authority; and as 'one of the venerators', he also continues to discover and make palpable objects, landscapes, creatures, in all their ordinariness and magicality.

Michael Longley's poetry, like Heaney's, has a wide range of cultural reference. In *No Continuing City* (1969), Circe, Nausicaä, Persephone and Narcissus rub shoulders with Walter Mitty, Emily Dickinson, John Clare, Dr Johnson, Rip Van Winkle, Fats Waller, Bud Freeman, Bessie Smith and Bix Beiderbecke, to mention only those who appear by name. These figures are brought into immediate relationship with the reader, technically through the use of apostrophe and dramatic monologue, but most profoundly in the way they come to represent the universally human. This and Longley's subsequent collections, which are less specifically allusive, illustrate his ability to approach his experience obliquely, through frameworks of myth, for example, or in a more directly personal manner, as in elegies such as 'Wounds', 'In Memoriam', and in his many delicate love poems. He is not so obsessively concerned with Irish history as are, say, Montague and Heaney, but he shows an awareness, especially in *An Exploded View* (1973), of cultural divisions in Ireland and of himself as an intellectual observer on the fringe of events; he does, however, affirm the importance of poetry as one of the reservoirs of positive, civilised values in time of chaos. World War I has always haunted his imagination as a part of family history and the robust elegies in which he exhumes and reburies his soldier father are both painful and vital. Among his adopted fathers are the war poets Edward Thomas, Isaac Rosenberg and Keith Douglas, all creative in the midst of destruction, all with an eye for the flora and fauna of the battlefield. Longely himself has a city dweller's love of birds, flowers, animals and landscapes, a love particularly evident in those poems set in the west of Ireland. He has translated and adapted memorably from the work of classical authors such as Homer and Tibullus, and his skill as a technician finds expression in the longer poem with elaborate stanza forms, the short poem that depends for its success on a few resonant images, and the verse letter.

Although Seamus Deane's first book, *Gradual Wars*, did not appear until 1972, he was a contemporary of Seamus Heaney's at Queen's University Belfast and Festival Publications had issued a pamphlet by him in 1966. *Gradual Wars* contains evocations of history-haunted, trouble-torn Derry, its recurrent persona a menaced figure among faces that loom out of nightmares, murderous shadows on the wall, the sounds and images of violence. Like the speaker in Heaney's 'The Tollund man', Deane finds himself 'lost, unhappy and at home', drawn to his native place but repelled by its injustices and corruption. His is an uneasy poetry of departure and homecoming, in which vulnerable, tenacious private lives are threatened by, and survive, the flux of history and in which emotion, intellect and imagination struggle to find order and repose among chaotic forces ultimately beyond their control.

11

Derek Mahon's poetry, too, is haunted by history and smitten with the restlessness of cities, the figures who inhabit it constantly in transit between life and death, control and chaos, one place and another. His confident wit and assured cadences function ironically as surface stabilities over unsettled depths but also as affirmations of art as a possible source of order, however inadequate, to set against all that is dauntingly 'unstructurable'. Mahon is particularly aware of the abyss that underlies the materialistic solidities of middle-class existence. He understands and identifies with the alienated – Ernest Dowson, Thomas De Quincey, Vincent Van Gogh, Edvard Munch, Malcolm Lowry, François Villon, Constantine Cavafy, Ovid, Knut Hamsun, Albert Camus – recognising how preferable to mindless complacency their lives can be, without sentimentalising their pain. Ireland usually figures in his poetry as a point of arrival or departure, a place from which he wishes to escape but which refuses to be exorcised, another ground on which he is drawn into the quest for equilibrium which informs his work, and into contemplation – especially in his collections *The Snow Party* (1975) and *The Hunt by Night* (1982) – of the vexed relationship between art and history. His vision of 'civilisation' in decline is balanced by an awareness of painful persistence and survival, the darkness in his poetry always struggling towards, or emerging into, its complement of light. He is the intelligent observer who realises the dangers of knowing too much 'to be anything any more', the elegist who, finally, refuses to mourn.

3

Poets from the north of Ireland have always sought publication for their poems and collections outside Belfast and a comprehensive list of their outlets would include the leading British and Irish journals and publishing houses of their periods. The first locally published magazine of any significance in the twentieth century was *Uladh* (1904–5), the organ of the Ulster Literary Theatre. The next two were *Lagan* (1943–6), edited by John Boyd, and *Rann* (1948–53), edited by Roy McFadden and

Barbara Hunter, both of which published, among others, MacNeice, Rodgers and Hewitt. *Threshold* was founded in 1957 and still appears sporadically. There have been, and are, numerous other platforms for poets, such as the *Northern Review*, *Everyman* (later called *Aquarius*), *Caret*, *Crab Grass*, *Fortnight*, *Gown*, the *Belfast Review* and *Rhinoceros*, but the only regular poetry magazine in recent times has been the *Honest Ulsterman*, first published in 1968. To date it has included not only the work of established northern poets but the first or early poems of Ciaran Carson, Michael Foley, Robert Johnstone, Medbh McGuckian, Tom Matthews, Paul Muldoon, Frank Ormsby, Tom Paulin, and William Peskett, and the first pamphlet collections of all these poets have appeared in the magazine's companion series, Ulsterman Publications. The most prominent local publisher of book-length collections is Blackstaff Press, founded in 1971; its list includes volumes by John Hewitt, Roy McFadden, Padraic Fiacc, John Montague, James Simmons, Michael Foley, Ciaran Carson, Robert Johnstone, Gerald Dawe and Andrew Elliott, and its *Trio* anthologies have introduced the work of numerous younger poets in book form.

If Tom Matthews's idiosyncratic poetry may be said to have a model, it is surely the work of the English poet, Stevie Smith. Beneath its deceptive spareness and simplicity, it is elusively alive to small sufferings, complexes, embarrassments, marginal alienations. It provides a refuge for such characters as Gustav the Great Explorer, who is not himself unless he has his snowboots on, Giorgio the Juggler from Bolton, whose audience applauds 'in desperation', the poet with bad teeth to whom an appearance-conscious public is not willing to listen. Matthews presents the lonely, the odd and the apparent failures in a way that sometimes tickles our sense of the absurd but stirs our sympathy as well.

Michael Foley, too, revels in the absurd, but less gently than Matthews. His viewpoint is often that of the wide-eyed, sharply watchful provincial-at-large, testing his preconceptions and expectations against experience. The poems in *True Life Love Stories* (1976) swing brashly between extravagant fantasy and an ironic self-debunking; they draw on such sources as film, comic-strip, jazz, colloquialism, journalese and literary quotation (accurate or deliberately adapted) for their headlong energy. Among the targets of Foley's iconoclastic humour are teachers and orthodox education, the tyranny of institutions, the pretentious and the stodgy, wherever they are found, the timidity of family and middle-class attitudes, materialism, social climbing. Some of the poems in *The GO Situation* (1982) make both satirical and affectionate use of managerial and other forms of jargon. In Foley the quiet voice associated with northern poetry turns sardonic, though he himself has described his 'loving mockery' as 'a kind of caress'. He is a poet who not only provokes the reader to uncomfortable self-assessment but invites him to 'delight in the usual', to sing the 'nooks and crannies of the day', to participate in 'the ragtime held in the soul'.

Foley helped edit the *Honest Ulsterman* magazine with Frank Ormsby. Ormsby's earliest work, which is set among the small farms and village housing estates of County Fermanagh, deals with the practicality and reticence of country people and their attachment to place, probing beneath the placid surfaces of their lives. In these poems, and also in his poems with Belfast settings, his awareness of division and upheaval is balanced by a desire to trust in human resilience, though he recognises that such trust is not always possible. He sees private lives both as blighted by public events and as flourishing toughly or serenely in spite of them. His second collection, *A Northern Spring* (1986), concerns visitors to and settlers in northern Ireland: American GIs, the Jewish, Chinese and Italian communities in Belfast, the 'Vietnamese boat-people of Portadown'.

City life in general, and the city of Belfast in particular, figures prominently in the poetry of Ciaran Carson, but especially in his collections *The Irish for No* (1987) and *Belfast Confetti* (1989). Carson's Belfast is an elusive, labyrinthine place. It has the solidity of brick and concrete but it is also a construct of memory and imagination, a city that disappears and renews itself daily. It is, furthermore, a bizarre, ominous place of codenamed undercover operations and the confidential telephone, of advanced surveillance technology, of bombings, murders and interrogations, a place where appearances cannot be trusted. Carson's poems are not, however, relentlessly grim. Several depict a beleaguered kind of normality, and in particular those illuminated by the dignity, imagination and humanity of his father intimate that future generations may inherit more than violence and division. Carson's densely textured, expansive poems, full of echoes and suggestive connections, amount to an impressive re-creation of urban history, folklore and mythology. Accumulating in long, deceptively prosaic lines that accommodate a range of detail and allusion, they extend and deepen our sense of place and challenge us to consider not only the nature of memory and imagination and the endless interrelationship of past and present but also the elusiveness and flexibility of language itself.

The people in Tom Paulin's poetry survive or pioneer in bleak, violent societies among the ruthless, divisive simplicities of politics, religion and class. They are often cautious and austere in their relationships – their security as much a matter of limitation as of safety. There is a harshness in many of Paulin's poems. Like Carson's, they re-create the concrete and steel realities of urban life. Paulin also depicts arid, oppressively masculine places, murderous cultures in which human behaviour is dominated by a lethal self-righteousness, and the ramshackle remnants of British colonialism. His third collection, *Liberty Tree* (1983), mourns the debasement of the radical, free-thinking, dissenting Presbyterianism that flourished in the north in the late eighteenth century, a phase of enlightenment cherished also by John Hewitt. Paulin's work is raw, contentious and urgent, animated by angry compassion, sardonic humour, fierce tenderness and an irrepressible vision of states and nations as they might be – reasonable, humane, 'unaggressively civilian'.

Medbh McGuckian is perhaps the most widely acclaimed Irish poet to have emerged in the 1980s. Many of her poems are set in an anonymous but sensuously realised, sometimes claustrophobic, world of houses, rooms, family and other relationships; others range outwards to incorporate the weather, the seasons, gardens, vegetation, the landscape and the planets in ways that are often symbolically significant. Her work is moodily intense, full of elusive anxieties and frustrations as well as a

15

shadowy eroticism; it fruitfully dramatises an obsession with the experience of being daughter, mother, lover, wife and poet. At their best, her lyrics and compressed narratives have a delicacy and richness of suggestion that escapes paraphrase; the reader is wooed into sharing fugitive feelings that a less-obliquely resonant approach might diminish, though the poems are sometimes so gnomic as to be impenetrable. The critic Kevin Barry defined one of McGuckian's essential qualities when he wrote that 'her poems work like a yeast, growing within their own process of writing'. Her voice is entirely individual, a memorably new sound in contemporary poetry.

Patrick Williams's *Trails* (1981), as its title suggests, may be read as a series of literal and metaphorical journeys along uncertain paths and half-roads. It is concerned with separations and distances, with travelling into the past, with leaving and returning to the poet's home town, Newcastle, County Down. It also maps the usually painful, occasionally joyous, progress towards wisdom, understanding and a sense of purpose. Williams catches the ache of small-town stagnation and the poignancy of timid, aimless lives, identifying with and kicking against the limitations of a provincial existence. He is angry for, and at, the people among whom he lives, impatient with their narrowness, for example, and their abject willingness to behave like underdogs, but recognising them as kin. His poetry is full of thwarted yearnings and aspirations, questionings and speculations, failures and cautious beginnings.

Robert Johnstone's first collection, *Breakfast in a Bright Room* (1983), introduces a serious poet with a sense of humour who writes with feeling, intelligence and imagination about a range of subjects: his father, his childhood in the Belfast suburb of Finaghy, his rural ancestry in County Tyrone, working in his father's grocery, summer holidays and summer jobs, and the experience of being in love. The sequel, *Eden to Edenderry* (1989), is a virtuoso performance, including, for instance, political satires and a sequence of fifteen interrelated sonnets set in Chelsea, where Johnstone now lives. He observes Northern Ireland from a distance as a kind of paradise lost that continues to engage his loyalty, affection and compassion. His strengths are particularly evident in a series of nine poems in which the sinking of the *Titanic* and the discovery of the wreck are a focus for haunting meditations on disaster and survival, politics and personal experience, dream and reality.

Paul Muldoon is probably the most inventive, resourceful and technically accomplished of the northern poets. He is a poet who relishes etymology, jokes, songs, stories and abstruse allusions, who revitalises idiom and cliché and manages language with a panache that few poets can rival. He is equally adept in the lyric, the sequence and the longer narrative poem. The sequences and narratives, which are difficult to represent by extract, offer sustained examples of his virtuosity and central concerns: 'Immram', for example, adapts the mythological 'Voyage of Muldoon' to the style of Raymond Chandler, parodying both in the process; in 'The more a man has, the more a man wants', based loosely on the Trickster Cycle of the Winnebago Indians, we accompany the hero Gallogly through a series of adventures that are by turns fantastical, farcical and a nightmarish panorama of violence in Northern Ireland; and in '7 Middagh Street' the thoughts of a group of artists who lived together briefly at that New York address in 1940 accumulate as a meditation on art, politics, sex and their interconnections. Muldoon's collections are characterised by a sly and – as one critic called it – 'whimful' brand of humour; each one offers a new voyage of exploration into the miraculously ordinary and the mundanely surreal.

The north of Gerald Dawe's *Sheltering Places* (1978) is urban and comprehensively 'Black' in its industrialisation and its violent inheritance from history. Blood, darkness and storm are as pervasive as in the poetry of Padraic Fiacc, and though emigration is considered as a possible means of escape, it is also seen as a kind of evasion. There is little consolation or ground for optimism in these poems. Northerners are, for instance, depicted as growing to accept their native place, but we are left with an impression of negative resignation as much as of active survival. The figures in Dawe's poetry tend to be haunted and rootless, on the move, bereft of certainties, their 'sheltering places' giving no guarantee of shelter, though in his subsequent collections *The Lundys Letter* (1985) and *Sunday School* (1990), the grimness of Dawe's vision is tempered by the warmth and trust of his domestic poems. He continues to explore the formative hinterland of the family and historical past in Northern Ireland, as well as the landscape, history and changing face of the west of Ireland, where he now lives.

William Peskett had, like Michael Foley, a scientific background, and it bears on his poems to an extent that Foley's does not. In *The Night-owl's Dissection* (1975), Peskett deals largely with detachment and impersonality. He depicts a clinical future in which the mysteries of the natural world (symbolised a number of times by the night-owl) may be diminished, casts a disenchanted eye on evolution and frequently contrasts the natural and the artificial. Peskett is aware and weary of the limitations of scientific knowledge and has a related affection and reverence for plants and animals. His protagonists are often insignificant figures, dwarfed by huge backdrops of history, time, the cosmos, though he has written some sprightly love poems. His second collection, *Survivors* (1980), develops the preoccupations of his first and also contains a number of poems that mark his move from Belfast to Suffolk.

The youngest poets in this anthology were born in the early 1960s when the present revival of northern poetry was also in its infancy. Peter McDonald was educated at Methodist College Belfast and Oxford. Andrew Elliott and John Hughes are only two members of a new wave of poets who attended Queen's University Belfast at a time when creative writing was fostered by a succession of writers-in-residence at both universities in Northern Ireland: John Hewitt, the dramatist Graham Reid, the American novelist William Wiser, Medbh McGuckian and James Simmons at Queen's; Derek Mahon, the dramatist Martin Lynch and the West Indian poet E.A. Markham at the University of Ulster. Selections of work by a number of these younger poets have appeared in the Blackstaff Press's *Trio* series and in the anthology *Map-Makers' Colours: New Poets of Northern Ireland*, edited by Todd Swift and Martin Mooney and published by Nu-Age Editions in Montreal in 1988.

Andrew Elliott is, first and foremost, a love poet. He is

18

fascinated by the strengths and vulnerabilities of women, their liberating influence, their openness to exploitation. Sometimes he gives these subjects an archetypal dimension through, for example, fairy tale; sometimes the treatment is more immediately personal. He is capable of sensitive self-projection into the experience of others and his assured rhythms, fastidious imagery and sense of humour give his collection *The Creationists* (1988) a quietly compelling quality. The mood of John Hughes's poetry is altogether harder and more forbidding. Many of the poems in *The Something in Particular* (1986) are tense, oblique narratives that draw their inspiration from a range of films and Hughes's characters move through a world where innocence – if it ever existed – has been left far behind, a world whose properties, as one reviewer remarked, are 'guns, sex, jealousy, blackmail, torture and perversion'. The poems are mainly fictions in which fantasy and illusion take on a distressing reality. Peter McDonald, too, draws images from the movies and employs a narrative mode. His subjects range from childhood in Belfast to the experiences of a prisoner in a Nazi concentration camp, from the Remembrance Day massacre in Enniskillen to money as religion and the heartlessness of high finance, from the precariousness of human relationships to the dehumanising effects of power. *Biting the Wax* (1989) has a composed, understated quality that serves to highlight the more ominous elements in the content but is characterised also by an inventive humour that alleviates the general bleakness of outlook. All three poets have learned from their elders – Elliott from Michael Longley, Hughes from Paul Muldoon, McDonald from Louis MacNeice and perhaps Longley and Tom Paulin – but all three have assimilated the influences and evolved a characteristic style.

4

The poets represented here have been praised for constant resourcefulness in the use of traditional forms, and accused of being technically unadventurous, unwilling to experiment, prisoners of the neat lyric. They have been commended for their restraint in not allowing the brutal realities of their place and time to impair their sense of aesthetic responsibility, and denounced for failure to 'confront' the realities directly. It has been said that their imaginative lives have, to an extent, been 'limited by the horizons defined by the colonial predicament' of the north and, on another level, that too many of them are 'insulated in some university shelter-belt or . . . ensconced in some cultural oasis such as the Arts Council or the BBC' and therefore cut off from the majority of ordinary lives. Their qualities of common sense and down-to-earthness have been approved as sources of strength, and deplored as factors that hold their imagination back from flight.

Readers must judge these matters for themselves. This edition of *Poets from the North of Ireland* celebrates the fact that an area once regarded as a cultural Siberia has nourished and continues to nourish a variety of poetic talents. It reflects the poets' shared concerns and individual preoccupations and their receptiveness to an enriching range of influences. Most importantly, perhaps, it is a gathering of poems which, for the most part, register, directly and obliquely, the time and place that produced them but which take us on rewarding journeys, home and away, from the provincial village to the global village, from the Moy to the universe.

GEORGE BUCHANAN

1904–1989

LYLE DONAGHY, POET, 1902–1949

The product of peoples on two sides of a narrow sea,
he was raised with his head full of half-naked Greeks.
His rainy countryside didn't, scholastically, exist.
Under a tree he heard drums with their heavy beat
recommend a dislike which he didn't share.

He watched from a window the rain splashing
and after the rain the treedrip on the river.
His poem, a slow adding of words,
grew with a lack of urgency as trees grow.
The mind exudes stuff, not in sentences
baked to a style, but softly. Sir,
I don't address you in precious stones.

He heard clergy shouting from pulpits against
the sins of the body. Schooled in the prime
material of flowering girls and trees,
he loved – poet-wise – poet-foolish –
with ex-puritan extravagance.

Turning a boulder in the grass, laughing
at the insects, he was filled with Whitman energy
as a train puffed by on the narrow-gauge.

Where do we go to find the evenings
which late sunshine on saplings used to make?
He piled stones savagely for a house for himself
in a valley, cautious about the trees,
not sinking to their calm, wanting to utter

a cry clear of the lake, an abstract
artifice beyond the natural liberties;
undid the academic ropes, waited for the surge.

CONVERSATION WITH STRANGERS

Strangers are people we haven't seen before,
the herbage of urban meadows. They're
unexplored countries. A greeting could expose
a fresh geography.

We open the door, go into the blue. The glance of others
is a sunlight. If we don't perceive them
we're without insight or sick. For everyone's invited
to be known: the new knowledge. It may be ignorance
that prevents us from loving our neighbours.

Too facile speaking betrays misery. We're sorry for gabblers
in a public place. We find it hard ourselves
to open our lips, being ponderous from past suffering.

We were reared in privacy, off the street, out of earshot.
'Oh no strangers, please! Only people we know!'

PRIVATE
KEEP OUT

This notice was pinned to the door. Let nobody look over the
    garden gate.
They also said: 'Don't refer to this or that in front of the child.'
                                        We became shy,
nervous of the great world. 'Don't speak to strangers,' they said.

It seemed starving strangers were waiting to catch at sensual
    straws, even
the unsatisfactory bodies of children.

Secrecy was praised. 'Don't visibly enjoy yourself. Find a hotel
apart from the crowd. Swim in a deserted bay. Be careful
what you say on the important subjects: better still, avoid them.
Give copious information on holidays, weather and sport; but
    hide your love
and your hate; seem to have a temperature of zero.'

Over against this was JC's message from Palestine
about loving people to whom we haven't been formally
    introduced.
Easiness with one another would show that the message
    is heard.
Citizens wouldn't be afraid of making asses of themselves.

Can we de-house and evict ourselves from our solid homes;
a break-out is due. Radio, newspaper,
pierce the shell of the house. Ah the relief
as the walls are pierced. Let's be unafraid
if the cameras come, if we're declared open to the public.

Like a girl on the stage who uncovers and states her
    essence,
we also expose ourselves: our naked fact is our unity.
All inhabitants are joined, even those who don't know it.
Those others are us; they must be hard to despise or kill.
We rear a joint city with a shared construction, hurrying
    builders, the tink of hammers.
But our ambition can come about only if we imagine our
    union.

Sneering at the sheer number of others is a drug for self-
    cultivators

who are also (they won't believe it) particles of the mass.
All of us are; and are filled with that million-made blaze.
Up it comes and burns through us.
As passengers of a train, shoppers, part of an audience,
we notice and are pleased to be with the rest.
Gone the bowing and scraping, the abject public, unworthy to
    come in.

The broken bigwigs, military heroes, so-called geniuses
are on show like deserted castles: a penny a peep!
The struggle to reclassify ourselves as top men or stars
isn't on. Our study isn't to reach a tower
but go deep like Orpheus into the general world,
to be unguarded with others.

In the park, please, no vilification of many in one place.
If we're world members we can't stiffen as others walk past us,
can't make faces of triumph or fear. Women sit in chairs; a
    grey-haired lady
shows her legs as one might mention a former wealth;
dandyish young lie under trees. There are bubbles
of affection in the long afternoon. The cold society
we used to know is almost dying. Strangers may cease to be
    strangers.
We may go to the park as to a room of (near) friends.

WAR-AND-PEACE

War is the angry man waving his desperate
    weapon,
the mushroom cloud in the Pacific Ocean.

Peace is quietude for retired persons sitting on
    fixed principles, sealed off from the climate of

26

the contingent in a place where nothing is
    urgent:
life arranged for academic study, isolated, sub-
    divided, known, a subject on which x and y
    may be taken as the recognised authorities.
It is that evening hymn full of tiredness and repose
    and low, stop-worrying voices, the reverend
    boredom.
It is an eternal luxury cruise in the sun with bingo
    at night after a heavy dinner.
Ideal circumstance, the advertised article, expensive
    ease:
a dream of summoning perfect waiters to the
    table with a small upward movement of
    the eyes.

There is neither war nor peace, there is war-*and*-
    peace, not either/or but the two:
rather, if you please, fusion, the play of one into
    the other, the blend.
War-and-peace isn't either anger or stillness, but
    persons moving in the great event of their
    city every day.
Not peace of mind but the troubled mind:
the warman on the peace path, the peaceman on
    the war path.
It is the impure joy, the dream and the awakening,
    the two sides of the medal:
the anxious holiday, the sunny tour of an Italian
    lake with a sick girl,
the extravagance of an unhappy time in a delectable
    but costly place,
friction in the country drawing room with an out-
    look of trees,
the senescence and poverty of a great public figure,

the evil politics of a new and exquisitely laid-out
    town.
It is co-operation with disliked persons, not segregation
    or party alignment,
but swallowing resentment, working with detested
    characters, undertaking a keen enterprise with
    untrustworthy associates;
talking of god's love with a bad-tempered clergy-
    man;
drinking a fine claret holding the glass with fingers from
    which torturers have drawn the nails;
coming home after dark to a divided family, living
    in harmony with a bitch.

I SUDDENLY . . .

I suddenly have come to love
you who have been no more than friend
so long and constantly . . .
                        I am
a traveller startled that the end
of stormy questing in a ship
for lands of mystery should be
to sight the blue smoke of his home
and anchor at his native quay.

SONG FOR STRAPHANGERS

I bought a red-brick villa
    and dug the garden round
because a young girl smiled in June:

28

in August we were bound
      by a marriage vow,
      and then till now
I count up every pound.

I count up every penny,
      I work and never cease,
because a young girl smiled in June
      and there is no release.
            Sometimes I swear
            it's most unfair.
Sometimes I feel at peace.

REVOLUTIONARY REVOLUTION

Insidious in ways no gunfire touches, revolution
must have revolution in it too,
not be the same old murder.

The cry for a tender
style has never been so truly from the heart,
so treated as nothing much.

THEATRICAL VENUS

She was the daughter of a fishmonger, she stood
bang in the middle of the audience-eye
for the woman she was, with all the best equipment:
the long full thighs, the erotic look
of one who wished to bring to the boil
the hidden gallons of blood in a thousand seated men.

She said: 'Men invent our attraction. Our hips were for us
  terra incognita
till audiences made us know the power of their discovery.'
The biological temperature went up, there was a tingle in the
  masculine zones,
but she, the prime mover, was unmoved,
as if she were alone in her bathroom stepping from a bath,
  swishing a towel.
She was being exceedingly private in public,
and this was her gift to the State.

A SPEAKER IN THE SQUARE

We hear her in the square. At two o'clock
fawn moths in thousands enter shops and cars.
There's a rush to shut the windows. Then
she steps to the platform without the brazen bearing
of usual parliament men. She can't do
miracles and sway the crowd; make listeners
advocates. She is heard
less for what she says than for her tossing
hair. Her love is to ideas,
the devastating love. Richness of feeling
is the prosperity she advocates.
'We won't permit a frozen future
or a manipulated one. Rebel.
Not by knifing constables, filling
the square with shots. No military coup.
Only a rise in temperature.
Freedom isn't freedom if people are cold.
Truth isn't truth if told by citizens
who don't care. We need an illumination
from glances. Human sunlight . . .'

Newspapers say it's true: WAR IS OFF.
For how long? History hasn't yet related.
Can the Prime Minister stay in office if
no war is threatened? He faces novel problems
when the electors aren't too deeply worried.
Without a mandate to be frivolous
he feels he must resign.

Author of elegant iambics, she
comes in a wintry moment, melts the ice
in a masculine country famous for reserve,
is carried to power by a flock of writers.
The Poetic State is founded.

JILL'S DEATH

After Jill died they remembered how she liked this chair,
her jokes about an ornament in the corner.
They did not trek mournfully to the cemetery
with its array of crosses at the border of the town.
They called some flowerbeds in the garden Jill's beds,
and said 'How are Jill's flowers today?' and went
outside and looked at them. The flowers swayed
or hardly moved in the slight wind. This
perfection spoke of the exact nature of life,
with undismayed joyfulness.

LEWIS MUMFORD

He has an eye for cities. Among his rows
of vegetables he dreams of cloistered squares
where people ruminate or meet without

being made nervous of a stream of cars.
This shocks the men who care for motor-speed
more than spontaneous interchange. They think
only a mind inadequately trained
would advocate a nice humanity.
But someone must, and he outstares the cynics.
The cause is worth it. His eager mind, employing
evidence from history, enters on
a massive disquisition to preserve
affectionate glances, tenderness in sips.

JOHN HEWITT

1907–1987

I WRITE FOR . . .

I write for my own kind,
I do not pitch my voice
that every phrase be heard
by those who have no choice:
their quality of mind
must be withdrawn and still,
as moth that answers moth
across a roaring hill.

ONCE ALIEN HERE

Once alien here my fathers built their house,
claimed, drained, and gave the land the shapes of use,
and for their urgent labour grudged no more
than shuffled pennies from the hoarded store
of well-rubbed words that had left their overtones
in the ripe England of the mounded downs.

The sullen Irish limping to the hills
bore with them the enchantments and the spells
that in the clans' free days hung gay and rich
on every twig of every thorny hedge,
and gave the rain-pocked stone a meaning past
the blurred engraving of the fibrous frost.

So I, because of all the buried men
in Ulster clay, because of rock and glen

and mist and cloud and quality of air
as native in my thought as any here,
who now would seek a native mode to tell
our stubborn wisdom individual,
yet lacking skill in either scale of song,
the graver English, lyric Irish tongue,
must let this rich earth so enhance the blood
with steady pulse where now is plunging mood
till thought and image may, identified,
find easy voice to utter each aright.

AN IRISHMAN IN COVENTRY

A full year since, I took this eager city,
the tolerance that laced its blatant roar,
its famous steeples and its web of girders,
as image of the state hope argued for,
and scarcely flung a bitter thought behind me
on all that flaws the glory and the grace
which ribbons through the sick, guilt-clotted legend
of my creed-haunted, godforsaken race.
My rhetoric swung round from steel's high promise
to the precision of the well-gauged tool,
tracing the logic in the vast glass headlands,
the clockwork horse, the comprehensive school.

Then, sudden, by occasion's chance concerted,
in enclave of my nation, but apart,
the jigging dances and the lilting fiddle
stirred the old rage and pity in my heart.
The faces and the voices blurring round me,
the strong hands long familiar with the spade,
the whiskey-tinctured breath, the pious buttons,
called up a people endlessly betrayed

by our own weakness, by the wrongs we suffered
in that long twilight over bog and glen,
by force, by famine and by glittering fables
which gave us martyrs when we needed men,
by faith which had no charity to offer,
by poisoned memory, and by ready wit,
with poverty corroded into malice,
to hit and run and howl when it is hit.

This is our fate: eight hundred years' disaster,
crazily tangled as the Book of Kells;
the dream's distortion and the land's division,
the midnight raiders and the prison cells.
Yet like Lir's children banished to the waters,
our hearts still listen for the landward bells.

THE SCAR

for Padraic Fiacc

There's not a chance now that I might recover
one syllable of what that sick man said,
tapping upon my great-grandmother's shutter,
and begging, I was told, a piece of bread;
for on his tainted breath there hung infection
rank from the cabins of the stricken west,
the spores from black potato-stalks, the spittle
mottled with poison in his rattling chest;
but she who, by her nature, quickly answered,
accepted in return the famine-fever;
and that chance meeting, that brief confrontation,
conscribed me of the Irishry for ever.

Though much I cherish lies outside their vision,
and much they prize I have no claim to share,
yet in that woman's death I found my nation;
the old wound aches and shews its fellow scar.

A FATHER'S DEATH

It was no vast dynastic fate
when gasp by gasp my father died,
no mourners at the palace gate,
or tall bells tolling slow and wide.

We sat beside the bed; the screen
shut out the hushed, the tiptoe ward,
and now and then we both would lean
to catch what seemed a whispered word.

My mother watched her days drag by,
two score and five the married years,
yet never weakened to a cry
who was so ready with her tears.

Then, when dawn washed the polished floor
and steps and voices woke and stirred
with wheels along the corridor,
my father went without a word.

The sick, the dying, bed by bed,
lay clenched around their own affairs;
that one behind a screen was dead
was someone's grief, but none of theirs.

It was no vast dynastic death,
no nation silent round that throne,
when, letting go his final breath,
a lonely man went out alone.

O COUNTRY PEOPLE

O country people, you of the hill farms,
huddled so in darkness I cannot tell
whether the light across the glen is a star,
or the bright lamp spilling over the sill,
I would be neighbourly, would come to terms
with your existence, but you are so far;
there is a wide bog between us, a high wall.
I've tried to learn the smaller parts of speech
in your slow language, but my thoughts need more
flexible shapes to move in, if I am to reach
into the hearth's red heart across the half-door.

You are coarse to my senses, to my washed skin;
I shall maybe learn to wear dung on my heel,
but the slow assurance, the unconscious discipline
informing your vocabulary of skill,
is beyond my mastery, who have followed a trade
three generations now, at counter and desk;
hand me a rake, and I at once, betrayed,
will shed more sweat than is needed for the task.

If I could gear my mind to the year's round,
take season into season without a break,
instead of feeling my heart bound and rebound
because of the full moon or the first snowflake,
I should have gained something. Your secret is pace.
Already in your company I can keep step,

but alone, involved in a headlong race,
I never know the moment when to stop.

I know the level you accept me on,
like a strange bird observed about the house,
or sometimes seen out flying on the moss
that may tomorrow, or next week, be gone,
liable to return without warning
on a May afternoon and away in the morning.
But we are no part of your world, your way,
as a field or a tree is, or a spring well.
We are not held to you by the mesh of kin;
we must always take a step back to begin,
and there are many things you never tell
because we would not know the things you say.

I recognise the limits I can stretch;
even a lifetime among you should leave me strange,
for I could not change enough, and you will not change;
there'd still be levels neither'd ever reach.
And so I cannot ever hope to become,
for all my good will toward you, yours to me,
even a phrase or a story which will come
pat to the tongue, part of the tapestry
of apt response, at the appropriate time,
like a wise saw, a joke, an ancient rime
used when the last stack's topped at the day's end,
or when the last lint's carted round the bend.

FROM THE TIBETAN

In my native province when I was young
the lamas were presumed to be dishonest,

38

not because they were more wicked than the rest
but their calling gave them more scope.

They were not expected to be philosophers
or poets, for they were not educated persons;
theories were as inconceivable as books
in their satchels. All they were asked
was to provide certain familiar noises
on fixed occasions of the calendar,
spinning the wheels with ritual fervour
and chanting of 'The Emperor's Tunic'
and 'The Great Wall of China'.

For the rest of their time it was anticipated
that they should work hard rewarding their families,
promoting their nephews, replenishing their stores,
and accepting presents from contractors.
Traditionally, all this was to be done with a show
of cordiality, with handclasps, salutes,
conspicuous finger-signals and audible passwords:
the effect which it was desired to produce
being that of reluctant necessity
for complicated manoeuvre.

Now I am older and live in the suburbs of the capital,
I find that the lamas here are very much the same,
save that the rewarding, promoting, replenishing, is
done on their behalf by a permanent secretariat,
leaving them more time to devote to the illusion
of exercising power: this forces them to acquire
a more sophisticated vocabulary; indeed,
one or two of them have written books:
in my native province this
would have been looked upon with disfavour,
for we are a simple people.

THE SEARCH

for Shirley and Darryl

We left the western island to live among strangers
in a city older by centuries
than the market town which we had come from
where the slow river spills out between green hills
and gulls perch on the bannered poles.

It is a hard responsibility to be a stranger;
to hear your speech sounding at odds with your neighbours';
holding your tongue from quick comparisons;
remembering that you are a guest in the house.

Often you will regret the voyage,
wakening in the dark night to recall that other place
or glimpsing the moon rising and recollecting
that it is also rising over named hills,
shining on known waters.

But sometimes the thought
that you have not come away from, but returned,
to this older place whose landmarks are yours also,
occurs when you look down a long street remarking
the architectural styles or move through a landscape
with wheat ripening in large fields.

Yet you may not rest here, having come back,
for this is not your abiding place, either.

The authorities declare that in former days
the western island was uninhabited,
just as where you reside now was once tundra,
and what you seek maybe no more than
a broken circle of stones on a rough hillside, somewhere.

BECAUSE I PACED MY THOUGHT

Because I paced my thought by the natural world,
the earth organic, renewed with the palpable seasons,
rather than the city falling ruinous, slowly
by weather and use, swiftly by bomb and argument,

I found myself alone who had hoped for attention.
If one listened a moment he murmured his dissent:
this is an idle game for a cowardly mind.
The day is urgent. The sun is not on the agenda.

And some who hated the city and man's unreasoning acts
remarked: He is no ally. He does not say that
Power and Hate are the engines of human treason.
There is no answering love in the yellowing leaf.

I should have made it plain that I stake my future
on birds flying in and out of the schoolroom window,
on the council of sunburnt comrades in the sun,
and the picture carried with singing into the temple.

THE RAM'S HORN

I have turned to the landscape because men disappoint me:
the trunk of a tree is proud, when the woodmen fell it,
it still has a contained ionic solemnity:
it is a rounded event without the need to tell it.

I have never been compelled to turn away from the dawn
because it carries treason behind its wakened face:
even the horned ram, glowering over the bog hole,
though symbol of evil, will step through the blown grass
    with grace.

Animal, plant, or insect, stone or water,
are, every minute, themselves; they behave by law.
I am not required to discover motives for them,
or strip my heart to forgive the rat in the straw.

I live my best in the landscape, being at ease there;
the only trouble I find I have brought in my hand.
See, I let it fall with a rustle of stems in the nettles,
and never for a moment suppose that they understand.

SUBSTANCE AND SHADOW

There is a bareness in the images
I temper time with in my mind's defence;
they hold their own, their stubborn secrecies;
no use to rage against their reticence:
a gannet's plunge, a heron by a pond,
a last rook homing as the sun goes down,
a spider squatting on a bracken-frond,
and thistles in a cornsheaf's tufted crown,
a boulder on a hillside, lichen-stained,
the sparks of sun on dripping icicles,
their durable significance contained
in texture, colour, shape, and nothing else.
All these are sharp, spare, simple, native to
this small republic I have charted out
as the sure acre where my sense is true,
while round its boundaries sprawl the screes of doubt.

My lamp lights up the kettle on the stove
and throws its shadow on the whitewashed wall,
like some Assyrian profile with, above,
a snake or bird-prowed helmet crested tall;

but this remains a shadow; when I shift
the lamp or move the kettle it is gone,
the substance and the shadow break adrift
that needed bronze to lock them, bronze or stone.

from SONNETS FOR ROBERTA (1954)

I

How have I served you? I have let you waste
the substance of your summer on my mood;
the image of the woman is defaced,
and some mere chattel-thing of cloth and wood
performs the household rites, while I, content,
mesh the fine words to net the turning thought,
or eke the hours out, gravely diligent,
to draw to sight that which, when it is brought,
is seldom worth the labour, while you wait,
the little loving gestures held at bay,
each mocking moment inappropriate
for pompous duty never stoops to play;
yet sometimes, at a pause, I recognise
the lonely pity in your lifted eyes.

II

If I had given you that love and care
I long have lavished with harsh loyalty
on some blurred concept spun of earth and air
and real only in some bird or tree,
then you had lived in every pulse and tone
and found the meaning in the wine and bread
who have been forced to walk these ways alone,
my dry thoughts droning always on ahead.
Then you had lived as other women live,

warmed by a touch, responsive to a glance,
glad to endure, so that endurance give
the right to share each changing circumstance,
and yet, for all my treason, you were true
to me, as I to something less than you.

A LOCAL POET

He followed their lilting stanzas
through a thousand columns or more,
and scratched for the splintered couplets
in the cracks on the cottage floor,
for his Rhyming Weavers fell silent
when they flocked through the factory door.

He'd imagined a highway of heroes
and stepped aside on the grass
to let Cuchullain's chariot through,
and the Starry Ploughmen pass;
but he met the Travelling Gunman
instead of the Gallowglass.

And so, with luck, for a decade
down the widowed years ahead,
the pension which crippled his courage
will keep him in daily bread,
while he mourns for his mannerly verses
that had left so much unsaid.

LOUIS MACNEICE

1907–1963

PRAYER BEFORE BIRTH

I am not yet born; O hear me.
Let not the bloodsucking bat or the rat or the stoat or the
    club-footed ghoul come near me.

I am not yet born, console me.
I fear that the human race may with tall walls wall me,
    with strong drugs dope me, with wise lies lure me,
        on black racks rack me, in blood baths roll me.

I am not yet born; provide me
With water to dandle me, grass to grow for me, trees to talk
    to me, sky to sing to me, birds and a white light
        in the back of my mind to guide me.

I am not yet born; forgive me
For the sins that in me the world shall commit, my words
    when they speak me, my thoughts when they think me,
        my treason engendered by traitors beyond me,
           my life when they murder by means of my
              hands, my death when they live me.

I am not yet born; rehearse me
In the parts I must play and the cues I must take when
    old men lecture me, bureaucrats hector me, mountains
        frown at me, lovers laugh at me, the white
           waves call me to folly and the desert calls
              me to doom and the beggar refuses
                my gift and my children curse me.

I am not yet born; O hear me,
Let not the man who is beast or who thinks he is God
    come near me.

I am not yet born; O fill me
With strength against those who would freeze my
    humanity, would dragoon me into a lethal automaton,
        would make me a cog in a machine, a thing with
            one face, a thing, and against all those
                who would dissipate my entirety, would
                    blow me like thistledown hither and
                        thither or hither and thither
                            like water held in the
                                hands would spill me.

Let them not make me a stone and let them not spill me.
Otherwise kill me.

CARRICKFERGUS

I was born in Belfast between the mountain and the gantries
    To the hooting of lost sirens and the clang of trams:
Thence to smoky Carrick in County Antrim
    Where the bottleneck harbour collects the mud which jams

The little boats beneath the Norman castle,
    The pier shining with lumps of crystal salt;
The Scotch Quarter was a line of residential houses
    But the Irish Quarter was a slum for the blind and halt.

The brook ran yellow from the factory stinking of chlorine,
    The yarn-mill called its funeral cry at noon;
Our lights looked over the lough to the lights of Bangor
    Under the peacock aura of a drowning moon.

The Norman walled this town against the country
    To stop his ears to the yelping of his slave
And built a church in the form of a cross but denoting
    The list of Christ on the cross in the angle of the nave.

I was the rector's son, born to the anglican order,
    Banned for ever from the candles of the Irish poor;
The Chichesters knelt in marble at the end of a transept
    With ruffs about their necks, their portion sure.

The war came and a huge camp of soldiers
    Grew from the ground in sight of our house with long
Dummies hanging from gibbets for bayonet practice
    And the sentry's challenge echoing all day long;

A Yorkshire terrier ran in and out by the gate lodge
    Barred to civilians, yapping as if taking affront:
Marching at ease and singing 'Who Killed Cock Robin?'
    The troops went out by the lodge and off to the Front.

The steamer was camouflaged that took me to England –
    Sweat and khaki in the Carlisle train;
I thought that the war would last for ever and sugar
    Be always rationed and that never again

Would the weekly papers not have photos of sandbags
    And my governess not make bandages from moss
And people not have maps above the fireplace
    With flags on pins moving across and across –

Across the hawthorn hedge the noise of bugles,
    Flares across the night,
Somewhere on the lough was a prison ship for Germans,
    A cage across their sight.

I went to school in Dorset, the world of parents
    Contracted into a puppet world of sons
Far from the mill girls, the smell of porter, the salt mines
    And the soldiers with their guns.

AUTOBIOGRAPHY

In my childhood trees were green
And there was plenty to be seen.

Come back early or never come.

My father made the walls resound,
He wore his collar the wrong way round.

Come back early or never come.

My mother wore a yellow dress;
Gentle, gently, gentleness.

Come back early or never come.

When I was five the black dreams came;
Nothing after was quite the same.

Come back early or never come.

The dark was talking to the dead;
The lamp was dark beside my bed.

Come back early or never come.

When I woke they did not care;
Nobody, nobody was there.

Come back early or never come.

When my silent terror cried,
Nobody, nobody replied.

Come back early or never come.

48

I got up; the chilly sun
Saw me walk away alone.

Come back early or never come.

SNOW

The room was suddenly rich and the great bay window was
Spawning snow and pink roses against it
Soundlessly collateral and incompatible:
World is suddener than we fancy it.

World is crazier and more of it than we think,
Incorrigibly plural. I peel and portion
A tangerine and spit the pips and feel
The drunkenness of things being various.

And the fire flames with a bubbling sound for world
Is more spiteful and gay than one supposes –
On the tongue on the eyes on the ears in the palms of one's
    hands –
There is more than glass between the snow and the huge roses.

from AUTUMN JOURNAL

XVI

Nightmare leaves fatigue:
    We envy men of action
Who sleep and wake, murder and intrigue
    Without being doubtful, without being haunted.

And I envy the intransigence of my own
  Countrymen who shoot to kill and never
See the victim's face become their own
  Or find his motive sabotage their motives.
So reading the memoirs of Maud Gonne,
  Daughter of an English mother and a soldier father,
I note how a single purpose can be founded on
  A jumble of opposites:
Dublin Castle, the vice-regal ball,
  The embassies of Europe,
Hatred scribbled on a wall,
  Gaols and revolvers.
And I remember, when I was little, the fear
  Bandied among the servants
That Casement would land at the pier
  With a sword and a horde of rebels;
And how we used to expect, at a later date,
  When the wind blew from the west, the noise of shooting
Starting in the evening at eight
  In Belfast in the York Street district;
And the voodoo of the Orange bands
  Drawing an iron net through darkest Ulster,
Flailing the limbo lands –
  The linen mills, the long wet grass, the ragged hawthorn.
And one read black where the other read white, his hope
  The other man's damnation:
Up the Rebels, To Hell with the Pope,
  And God Save – as you prefer – the King or Ireland.
The land of scholars and saints:
  Scholars and saints my eye, the land of ambush,
Purblind manifestos, never-ending complaints,
  The born martyr and the gallant ninny;
The grocer drunk with the drum,
  The landowner shot in his bed, the angry voices
Piercing the broken fanlight in the slum,
  The shawled woman weeping at the garish altar.

Kathleen ni Houlihan! Why
   Must a country, like a ship or a car, be always female,
Mother or sweetheart? A woman passing by,
   We did but see her passing.
Passing like a patch of sun on the rainy hill
   And yet we love her for ever and hate our neighbour
And each one in his will
   Binds his heirs to continuance of hatred.
Drums on the haycock, drums on the harvest, black
   Drums in the night shaking the windows:
King William is riding his white horse back
   To the Boyne on a banner.
Thousands of banners, thousands of white
   Horses, thousands of Williams
Waving thousands of swords and ready to fight
   Till the blue sea turns to orange.
Such was my country and I thought I was well
   Out of it, educated and domiciled in England,
Though yet her name keeps ringing like a bell
   In an underwater belfry.
Why do we like being Irish? Partly because
   It gives us a hold on the sentimental English
As members of a world that never was,
   Baptised with fairy water;
And partly because Ireland is small enough
   To be still thought of with a family feeling,
And because the waves are rough
   That split her from a more commercial culture;
And because one feels that here at least one can
   Do local work which is not at the world's mercy
And that on this tiny stage with luck a man
   Might see the end of one particular action.
It is self-deception of course;
   There is no immunity in this island either;
A cart that is drawn by somebody else's horse

And carrying goods to somebody else's market.
The bombs in the turnip sack, the sniper from the roof,
Griffith, Connolly, Collins, where have they brought us?
Ourselves alone! Let the round tower stand aloof
In a world of bursting mortar!
Let the school children fumble their sums
In a half-dead language;
Let the censor be busy on the books; pull down the
Georgian slums;
Let the games be played in Gaelic.
Let them grow beet-sugar; let them build
A factory in every hamlet;
Let them pigeonhole the souls of the killed
Into sheep and goats, patriots and traitors.
And the North, where I was a boy,
Is still the North, veneered with the grime of Glasgow,
Thousands of men whom nobody will employ
Standing at the corners, coughing.
And the street children play on the wet
Pavement – hopscotch or marbles;
And each rich family boasts a sagging tennis net
On a spongy lawn beside a dripping shrubbery.
The smoking chimneys hint
At prosperity round the corner
But they make their Ulster linen from foreign lint
And the money that comes in goes out to make more
money.
A city built upon mud;
A culture built upon profit;
Free speech nipped in the bud,
The minority always guilty.
Why should I want to go back
To you, Ireland, my Ireland?
The blots on the page are so black
That they cannot be covered with shamrock.

I hate your grandiose airs,
    Your sob-stuff, your laugh and your swagger,
Your assumption that everyone cares
    Who is the king of your castle.
Castles are out of date,
    The tide flows round the children's sandy fancy;
Put up what flag you like, it is too late
    To save your soul with bunting.
Odi atque amo:
    Shall we cut this name on trees with a rusty dagger?
Her mountains are still blue, her rivers flow
    Bubbling over the boulders.
She is both a bore and a bitch;
    Better close the horizon,
Send her no more fantasy, no more longings which
    Are under a fatal tariff.
For common sense is the vogue
    And she gives her children neither sense nor money
Who slouch around the world with a gesture and a brogue
    And a faggot of useless memories.

THE SUNLIGHT ON THE GARDEN

The sunlight on the garden
Hardens and grows cold,
We cannot cage the minute
Within its nets of gold,
When all is told
We cannot beg for pardon.

Our freedom as free lances
Advances towards its end;
The earth compels, upon it

53

Sonnets and birds descend;
And soon, my friend,
We shall have no time for dances.

The sky was good for flying
Defying the church bells
And every evil iron
Siren and what it tells:
The earth compels,
We are dying, Egypt, dying

And not expecting pardon,
Hardened in heart anew,
But glad to have sat under
Thunder and rain with you,
And grateful too
For sunlight on the garden.

MEETING-POINT

Time was away and somewhere else,
There were two glasses and two chairs
And two people with the one pulse
(Somebody stopped the moving stairs):
Time was away and somewhere else.

And they were neither up nor down;
The stream's music did not stop
Flowing through heather, limpid brown,
Although they sat in a coffee shop
And they were neither up nor down.

The bell was silent in the air
Holding its inverted poise –

Between the clang and clang a flower,
A brazen calyx of no noise:
The bell was silent in the air.

The camels crossed the miles of sand
That stretched around the cups and plates;
The desert was their own, they planned
To portion out the stars and dates;
The camels crossed the miles of sand.

Time was away and somewhere else.
The waiter did not come, the clock
Forgot them and the radio waltz
Came out like water from a rock:
Time was away and somewhere else.

Her fingers flicked away the ash
That bloomed again in tropic trees:
Not caring if the markets crash
When they had forests such as these,
Her fingers flicked away the ash.

God or whatever means the Good
Be praised that time can stop like this,
That what the heart has understood
Can verify in the body's peace
God or whatever means the Good.

Time was away and she was here
And life no longer what it was,
The bell was silent in the air
And all the room one glow because
Time was away and she was here.

THE INTRODUCTION

They were introduced in a grave glade
And she frightened him because she was young
And thus too late. Crawly crawly
Went the twigs above their heads and beneath
The grass beneath their feet the larvae
Split themselves laughing. Crawly crawly
Went the cloud above the treetops reaching
For a sun that lacked the nerve to set
And he frightened her because he was old
And thus too early. Crawly crawly
Went the string quartet that was tuning up
In the back of the mind. You two should have met
Long since, he said, or else not now.
The string quartet in the back of the mind
Was all tuned up with nowhere to go.
They were introduced in a green grave.

ELEGY FOR MINOR POETS

Who often found their way to pleasant meadows
Or maybe once to a peak, who saw the Promised Land,
Who took the correct three strides but tripped their hurdles,
Who had some prompter they barely could understand,
Who were too happy or sad, too soon or late,
I would praise these in company with the Great;

For if not in the same way, they fingered the same language
According to their lights. For them as for us
Chance was a coryphaeus who could be either
An angel or an *ignus fatuus*.
Let us keep our mind open, our fingers crossed;
Some who go dancing through dark bogs are lost.

Who were lost in many ways, through comfort, lack of
    knowledge,
Or between women's breasts, who thought too little, too much,
Who were the world's best talkers, in tone and rhythm
Superb, yet as writers lacked a sense of touch,
So either gave up or just went on and on –
Let us salute them now their chance is gone;

And give the benefit of the doubtful summer
To those who worshipped the sky but stayed indoors
Bound to a desk by conscience or by the spirit's
Hay fever. From those office and study floors
Let the sun clamber on to the notebook, shine,
And fill in what they groped for between each line.

Who were too carefree or careful, who were too many
Though always few and alone, who went the pace
But ran in circles, who were lamed by fashion,
Who lived in the wrong time or the wrong place,
Who might have caught fire had only a spark occurred,
Who knew all the words but failed to achieve the Word –

Their ghosts are gagged, their books are library flotsam,
Some of their names – not all – we learnt in school
But, life being short, we rarely read their poems,
Mere source-books now to point or except a rule,
While those opinions which rank them high are based
On a wish to be different or on lack of taste.

In spite of and because of which, we later
Suitors to their mistress (who, unlike them, stays young)
Do right to hang on the grave of each a trophy
Such as, if solvent, he would himself have hung
Above himself; these debtors preclude our scorn –
Did we not underwrite them when we were born?

THE TRUISMS

His father gave him a box of truisms
Shaped like a coffin, then his father died;
The truisms remained on the mantelpiece
As wooden as the playbox they had been packed in
Or that other his father skulked inside.

Then he left home, left the truisms behind him
Still on the mantelpiece, met love, met war,
Sordor, disappointment, defeat, betrayal,
Till through disbeliefs he arrived at a house
He could not remember seeing before,

And he walked straight in; it was where he had come from
And something told him the way to behave.
He raised his hand and blessed his home;
The truisms flew and perched on his shoulders
And a tall tree sprouted from his father's grave.

THE TAXIS

In the first taxi he was alone tra-la,
No extras on the clock. He tipped ninepence
But the cabby, while he thanked him, looked askance
As though to suggest someone had bummed a ride.

In the second taxi he was alone tra-la
But the clock showed sixpence extra; he tipped according
And the cabby from out of his muffler said: 'Make sure
You have left nothing behind tra-la between you.'

In the third taxi he was alone tra-la
But the tip-up seats were down and there was an extra

Charge of one-and-sixpence and an odd
Scent that reminded him of a trip to Cannes.

As for the fourth taxi, he was alone
Tra-la when he hailed it but the cabby looked
Through him and said: 'I can't tra-la well take
So many people, not to speak of the dog.'

CHARON

The conductor's hands were black with money:
Hold on to your ticket, he said, the inspector's
Mind is black with suspicion, and hold on to
That dissolving map. We moved through London,
We could see the pigeons through the glass but failed
To hear their rumours of wars, we could see
The lost dog barking but never knew
That his bark was as shrill as a cock crowing,
We just jogged on, at each request
Stop there was a crowd of aggressively vacant
Faces, we just jogged on, eternity
Gave itself airs in revolving lights
And then we came to the Thames and all
The bridges were down, the further shore
Was lost in fog, so we asked the conductor
What we should do. He said: Take the ferry
Faute de mieux. We flicked the flashlight
And there was the ferryman just as Virgil
And Dante had seen him. He looked at us coldly
And his eyes were dead and his hands on the oar
Were black with obols and varicose veins
Marbled his calves and he said to us coldly:
If you want to die you will have to pay for it.

W.R. RODGERS

1909–1969

WORDS

Always the arriving winds of words
Pour like Atlantic gales over these ears,
These reefs, these foils and fenders, these shrinking
And sea-scalded edges of the brain-land.
Rebutted and rebounding, on they post
Past my remembrance, falling all unplanned.
But some day out of darkness they'll come forth,
Arrowed and narrowed into my tongue's tip,
And speak for me – their most astonished host.

THE LOVERS

After the tiff there was stiff silence, till
One word, flung in centre like single stone,
Starred and cracked the ice of her resentment
To its edge. From that stung core opened and
Poured up one outward and widening wave
Of eager and extravagant anger.

STORMY NIGHT

Is this the street? Never a sign of life,
The swinging lamp throws everything about;
But see! from that sly doorway, like a knife
The gilt edge of inviting light slides out

And in again – the very sign
Of her whose slightest nod I lately thought was mine;

But not now.
Knock! and the night-flowering lady
Opens, and across the brilliant sill
Sees me standing there so dark and shady
Hugging the silences of my ill will;
Wildly she turns from me – But no, my love,
This foot's within the door, this hand's without the glove.

Well may you tremble now, and say there was nothing
     meant,
And curl away from my care with a 'Please, my dear!'
For though you were smoke, sucked up by a raging vent,
I'd follow you through every flue of your fear,
And over your faraway arms I'll mountain and cone
In a pillar of carolling fire and fountaining stone.

O strike the gong of your wrong, raise the roof of your rage,
Fist and foist me off with a cloud of cries,
What do I care for all your footling rampage?
On your light-in-gale blows my larking caresses will rise,
But – Why so still? What! are you weeping, my sweet?
Ah heart, heart, look! I throw myself at your feet.

THE NET

Quick, woman, in your net
Catch the silver I fling!
O I am deep in your debt,
Draw tight, skintight, the string,
And take the silver in.

No fisher ever yet
Drew such a cunning ring.

Ah, shifty as the fin
Of any fish this flesh
That, shaken to the shin,
Now shoals into your mesh,
Bursting to be held in;
Purse-proud and pebble-hard,
Its pence like shingle showered.

Open the haul, and shake
The fill of shillings free,
Let all the satchels break
And leap about the knee
In shoals of ecstasy.
Guineas and gills will flake
At each gull-plunge of me.

Though all the angels, and
Saint Michael at their head,
Nightly contrive to stand
On guard about your bed,
Yet none dare take a hand,
But each can only spread
His eagle-eye instead.

But I, being man, can kiss
And bed-spread-eagle too;
All flesh shall come to this,
Being less than angel is,
Yet higher far in bliss
As it entwines with you.

Come, make no sound, my sweet;
Turn down the candid lamp

And draw the equal quilt
Over our naked guilt.

LENT

Mary Magdalene, that easy woman,
Saw, from the shore, the seas
Beat against the hard stone of Lent,
Crying, 'Weep, seas, weep
For yourselves that cannot dent me more.

'O more than all these, more crabbed than all stones,
And cold, make me, who once
Could leap like water, Lord. Take me
As one who owes
Nothing to what she was. Ah, naked.

'My waves of scent, my petticoats of foam
Put from me and rebut;
Disown. And that salt lust stave off
That slavered me – O
Let it whiten in grief against the stones

'And outer reefs of me. Utterly doff,
Nor leave the lightest veil
Of feeling to heave or soften.
Nothing cares this heart
What hardness crates it now or coffins.

'Over the balconies of these curved breasts
I'll no more peep to see
The light procession of my loves
Surf-riding in to me
Who now have eyes and alcove, Lord, for Thee.'

63

'Room, Mary,' said He, 'ah make room for me
Who am come so cold now
To my tomb.' So, on Good Friday,
Under a frosty moon
They carried Him and laid Him in her womb.

A grave and icy mask her heart wore twice,
But on the third day it thawed,
And only a stone's-flow away
Mary saw her God.
Did you hear me? Mary saw her God!

Dance, Mary Magdalene, dance, dance and sing,
For unto you is born
This day a King. 'Lady,' said He,
'To you who relent
I bring back the petticoat and the bottle of scent.'

THE SWAN

Bottomed by tugging combs of water
The slow and loath swan slews and looks
Coldly down through chutes of stilled chatter
Upon the shadows in flight among the stones.

Into abashed confusions of ooze
It dips, and from the muddy fume
The silver and flute-like fishes rise
Endlessly up through all their octaves of gloom

To where the roofed swan suavely swings
Without qualm on the quivering wave
That laves it on, with elbowing wings held wide
Under its eyes' hugged look and architrave.

Jonquil-long its neck adjudicates
Its body's course; aloof and cool
It cons the nonchalant and unseeing air
With its incurious and dispassionate stare.

Slow, slow, it slides, as if not to chafe
The even sleeve of its approach
Stretched stiff and oval in front of it,
Siphoning it on, selfless, silent, and safe.

On that grey lake, frilled round with scufflings
Of foam and milled with muttering
I saw lingering, late and lightless,
A single swan, swinging, sleek as a sequin.

Negligently bright, wide wings pinned back,
It mooned on the moving water,
And not all the close and gartering dark
Or gathering wind could lift or flatter
That small and dimming image into flight;
Far from shore and free from foresight,
Coiled in its own indifferent mood
It held the heavens, shores, waters and all their brood.

THE PARTY

So they went, leaving a picnic-litter of talk
And broken glitter of jokes, the burst bags of spite:
In comes Contempt the caretaker, eye on ceiling,
Broom in armpit, and with one wide careless cast
Sweeps the stuttering rubbish out of memory,
Opens the shutters, puts out the intimate lamp,
And, a moment, gazes on the mute enormities
Of distant dawn. And far doors bang in mind, idly.

65

from RESURRECTION: AN EASTER SEQUENCE

Then cometh Jesus with them unto a place called Gethsemane.

It was a lovely night,
A night for weddings and for water.
Going out into the cold glow he felt washed
And clean of people. The garden had an air
Of waiting about it, as if the leaves were bent
On eavesdropping. And the rain
Scented the air with more-than-midnight pain
And the wet trees that had nowhere to go
Stood round and gazed at the One walking there below
In agony. Ebb and flow, to and fro, Yes and No;
Doubt assailed him. Which and what to do? This much must be
    admitted,
We live between two worlds, faith and doubt,
Like breath. The air that one breathes does not care
Whether it's in or out; it's not in love with life
Or death. And yet we do not dare to hold it long,
But must let go to find again. So with faith,
With love, with everything. Now at the crossroads,
Middled and muddled he stood.
This was it. And it was night. 'Nevertheless Thy will be done.'
That thought made morning of it, gave him ease, and issue.
He knew now how to stay and stare it out
And already the torches approached the garden . . .

And when he had scourged Jesus, he delivered him to be crucified.

They took him out to die.
The lark was shaking out its acres of song in the sky
And the sun shone. People looked up and remarked
What a wonderful day it was going to be
And the cheering boys ran on in front of the crowd,
And the cheeky ones waited to stare.

66

                                        Once he noticed
A blind man whom he had healed looking at him
With horrified eyes as much as to say
'Was it for this I was given sight by the god that day?'
He turned away. If only this had been an important death,
If only he knew that the people who barracked him now
Had been travelling years and years to reach this place.
But they were casual passers-by and their interest was jaded.
Yet it was all as he had expected, and
He would not avoid or evade it. Far away
A spool of birds was spinning above the hill,
And still Pilate sat in the empty court beneath,
Sucking threads of thoughtfulness through his teeth.

And they crucified him.

This was a rough death, there was nothing tidy about it,
No sweetness, nothing noble.
Everything stuck out awkwardly and angular:
The clumsy soldier brought the wrong basket of nails;
And the couriers – those sticky fly-papers of events –
Did not even bother to cover his sticky end,
Or carry it home to Rome. For them the war in Gaul
Was more important; the ship of state sailed on,
Leaving him bogging in the backward seas.
Still, that is how things always happen, lousily,
But later on, the heart edits them lovingly,
Abstracts the jeers and jags, imports a plan
Into the pain, and calls it history.
We always go back to gloss over some roughness,
To make the past happen properly as we want it to happen.
But this was a hard death. At the time
There was no room for thought.
How often he had hearsed and rehearsed this hour.
But when you come up against it all the good words about it
Are less than breath. It is hard to turn the other cheek

When both have been slapped:
                              Yes, it was a hard death.

Now there stood by the Cross of Jesus his mother . . .

A mist opened and closed its eyes before him,
And in it he saw her looking at him,
The untouchable terrible god.
O what ladders of longing led up from her
To him, what steps and depths of memory ran down;
He remembered the happy days in Galilee
When he was heaven's hub; the heap of smoking grass,
The bubble-pipe, the light upon the wall,
The children in the far garden looking for the lost ball,
And Mary calling him. He was always so distant
In those lonely days. O if only
He had mattered less, she wondered, if only
She had mastered him more, would he then
Have been like other men, a flat satisfied plain?
But no. In him mountains of onlyness rose
Snow-high. Dayspring was in his eyes
At midnight. And he would not come down
From his far purpose even for her who was
The root that raised him to this Cross and crown
Of thorns. Yet tenderly he spoke
Goodbye now, his voice choking and dry.
And as she went away, leaving him to die,
The vast moon of his cry rose up upon the darkness.
His heart broke . . .

And there was Mary Magdalene and the other Mary, sitting over
    against the sepulchre . . .

It is always the women who are the Watchers
And Keepers of life, they guard our exits
And our entrances. They are both tomb and womb,

End and beginning. Bitterly they bring forth
And bitterly take back the light they gave.
The last to leave and still the first to come.
They circle us like sleep or like the grave.
Earth is their element, and in it lies
The seed and silence of the lighted skies,
The seasons with their fall and slow uprise,
Man with his sight and militant surmise.
It is always the women who are the Watchers
And Wakeners . . .

FIELD DAY

The old farmer, nearing death, asked
To be carried outside and set down
Where he could see a certain field
'And then I will cry my heart out,' he said.

It troubles me, thinking about that man;
What shape was the field of his crying
In Donegal?

I remember a small field in Down, a field
Within fields, shaped like a triangle.
I could have stood there and looked at it
All day long.

And I remember crossing the frontier between
France and Spain at a forbidden point, and seeing
A small triangular field in Spain,
And stopping

Or walking in Ireland down any rutted by-road
To where it hit the highway, there was always

At this turning-point and abutment
A still centre, a V-shape of grass
Untouched by cornering traffic,
Where country lads larked at night.

I think I know what the shape of the field was
That made the old man weep.

ROBERT GREACEN

b. 1920

THE BIRD

A bird flew tangent-wise to the open window.
His face was a black face of black, unknowing death;
His eyes threw the grim glint of sharpened stones
That children pile by unfrequented roads.

And that night, dreaming into a rapture of cardboard life,
I stared at the lean face of the bird:
A crow I think it was, but it was also death
And sure enough there was the crisp telegram next morning.

I placed my mirror to the flat, unfiltered light
But the razor cut me in spite of the guarantee,
And I knew it was not the razor but the ebony beak
That slashed the base of my left nostril.

I loved the man who lay in the cheap coffin.
It was he first showed me the damp, stereoscopic fields
Of County Down – and now he was away to farm
The curving acres of his jealous God.

I loved the ploughing of his sun-caught brow,
And the hay-lines and the chicken feathers in his hair
That was hay itself, the strongly cobbled boots
And the swaying, coloured idiom of his mind.

And now he was lying with the Holy Bible under his chin,
Sorry only to have died before harvest and turf-cutting,
Lying dead in the room of rafters and the grey, stopped clock –
Because of the hatred of the bird I did not kill.

Sometimes now, years after, I am nakedly afraid in
   midwinter
And ashamed to be afraid of an incessant beak
That raps a symphony of death on the window panes
Of the window I dare not throw wide open.

But one evening, just before I go to bed to die,
There will be the black face of black, unknowing death
Flying past my open window; there will be the black bird
With poison in his beak and hatred in his wings.

FATHER AND SON

I can't remember how it happened,
How hatred seeded and grew rank,
A tall weed that dwarfed us both
And flourished till it stank.

Yet that isn't the whole story.
I remember evenings when, father and son,
We walked the velvety spring streets
And greeted the blossoms one by one.

Images come blurred, then clear
To harshness, violence; but still
Behind the bitter word, the angry gesture,
I find the love that neither wished to kill.

Rest in peace, my father, trespass forgiven,
The dark stains whitened out. Today
The siren screams our armistice,
The angry dwarfs ride fast away.

A SUMMER DAY

Dream of a summer day: a hearse,
Bleached tombstones, gold letters glinting.
A stone forest in a city suburb.
Beloved husband, much-loved son,
Thy will, O Lord, not ours be done.
Mother in the oak coffin; yes, at last
After much pain and long, hard years
That came to nearly eighty-eight.
Voiceless I stand, her often wayward boy,
While the minister intones grave words
I hear but don't quite grasp:
'Receive Elizabeth, Thy servant here.'
Sweetest of names, Elizabeth,
Each syllable a childhood bell.
Dismay and guilt in this neat wilderness,
I don't know where to turn my head.
Down, down, down. Wood unto earth.
Gravediggers tipped. All smoothly done.
Back now to the shining city
And the Victorians round the City Hall
Frozen for ever in their sooty marble.
Gone, gone, gone, gone. All gone.
Back from the rectangles of the quiet dead.
Back to memory and guilt. Back to dismay.
Back to the nightmare of a summer day.

CAPTAIN FOX

Captain Fox sits reading metaphysics,
Hegel's the hundred-watt bulb in his world.
Captain Fox is fond of Zurich's Hotel Excelsior.

'A reliable place,' he says, 'solid, reliable.'
He lights a Gauloise and blows a ring:
'One of these days I'll retire, I'm getting too old
For buggering along the autobahns.
Besides, I want to write a pre-Ayer work on philosophy
Which I'll publish at my own expense.
"Aspects of Hegel" or some such title.
Perhaps a village on the Adriatic . . .'

Basques, Catalans, Slovaks, Irishmen, Blacks,
These are Captain Fox's friends
Or perhaps, more exactly, business associates.
Luckily he's as much linguist as philosopher.
He talks for hours about fireworks
And the poetry of Rainer Maria Rilke.
Truly a civilised man, Captain Fox.

'Are you in business?' I once asked him.
'Well, let's say I provide . . . facilities.'
A most civilised man, Captain Fox,
Discreet, solid, reliable.

His business isn't my business.

ST ANDREW'S DAY

St Andrew's Day, blind November fumbling
The hurt leaves, bleached gutter orphans.
Half-light domesticates raw brick.
A mediocre day, not to be remembered.
It's 2 p.m. at Ladbroke Grove. I board a bus.
The mourners are gathering at Glenariff.
Is it drizzling there? I hear the rain
Touch-typing an elegy on the Bay waters.

Though in her will she said 'no flowers'
Our daughter will place veronica on the coffin
Borne through the woods to the Old Killeen.
Will the funeral go to plan, discreetly,
Even in the drizzle I imagine falling
On the lands of Gael and Planter?
I say a London goodbye to a lost wife,
Remember our time of roses, promises,
The silvered sea at Ardnagashel,
Earrings of fuchsia in the hedgerows,
Hope arching like a rainbow over all.

CARNIVAL AT THE RIVER

The procession of ghosts shuffles by,
Faceless, bannerless, blobs in a landscape
Of dead trees, rotted flowers.
Gradually the blobs dissolve into people.
Father steps out in Edwardian style,
Links arms with Mother in her flowered hat.
There's cousin Jim, his gun lusting for snipe.
Aunt Tillie's fox fur dangles at her neck.
Teachers pace by in funereal gowns,
Boys in uniform, bare-kneed, sulk past
As if they'd been cheated of a holiday.
Stewart pushes a 1930s Raleigh bike,
Willie McIlwaine drools over an oval ball.
I turn on my side and hope for easy sleep
Away from the images of childhood
But the procession sidles into dream.
I am walking beside Grandfather.
He plucks his goatee, tells me softly:
'We're going to the carnival.

We are gathering at the river.'
I feel cold, my guts tighten.
Father's father, take my arm!
Grandfather holds me, quotes Beckett:
'Je n'ai rien contre les cimetières.'
We laugh, walk arm in arm to the carnival,
The gathering at the river.

ROY MCFADDEN

b. 1921

EPITHALAMIUM

So you are married, girl. It makes me sad
At heart to think that you, last summer held
Between hot hands on slow white afternoons,
Whose eyes I knew down to their blackest depths
(Stirred by the indolent smile and the quick laugh)
Are married now. Some man whom I have not seen
Calls up the smile and the laugh, holds in his hands
The welcoming body, sees in the darkening eyes
Sufficient future in a shaded room.
I wish you well. Now, with twin-set and pearls,
Your girlhood gone, that summer on your skin,
You'll settle down, keep up appearances.
I, wed to history, pray for your peace;
That the smile be never twisted in your mouth,
And the pond of your mind never be rippled with sorrow:
That you may sleep your sleep as the world quakes,
And never see the chasms at your feet.

from MEMORIES OF CHINATOWN

BIGAMY

His cycle kerbed, the peeler found
The lad behind the door, the girl
Biting her flowered pinafore,
Hushed neighbours aching for a sound.

He went off with the constable,
Cap wedged inside his pocket with
A blackened butt and one red match,
And helped to push the bicycle.

The girl stole in and closed the blinds.
Neighbours stormed to angry pans
And urgent irons' climbing steam,
Straitlaced within their marriage-lines.

But no one chased the constable
To ask what harm the lad had done
In kindling love on her cold hearth;
Or who would be accountable

For her trousseau of cast-off love,
Her honeymoon arrested, ring
And name flung off, her shame
A thumb in a burst glove.

CONTEMPLATIONS OF MARY

1

When he said *Mary*, she did not at once
Look up to find the voice, but sat recalling
Warm patches of her childhood, and her falling
Heart-over-head in love with every glance
Of admiration crowding through the dance,
Or in the streets bent back and almost calling.

Girls put on sex like flowers; nascent breasts
Emerge like blushes, knowing, innocent;
The underflow of all their ways intent

On welling up with welcome for the guests
Who darken love's white threshold. All the rest's
Above, outside, like god and government.

So she sat on when he first spoke to her.
Hearing perhaps a new sound of command,
Like parent's tug at child's reluctant hand,
Did not at once look up and answer *Sir*,
But sat with memory her conspirator,
Downcast, and did not want to understand.

But he persisted. *Mary.* She resigned
Her meadows and her rainbows to his voice,
Inevitably now, without a choice,
Surrendering all the stairways of her mind;
Then, finally bereft, was empty, blind,
Until the word bulged up and broke. *Rejoice.*

2

Then she was different. Her past perfect years
Seemed like another woman's purse, all strange
In ordinary things, keys, compact, change:
And home no longer nested up those stairs,
Involved with tables, pictures, cupboards, chairs.

Now everything was leaning out askew
Since it had touched, no hardly touched her, blown
A strange breath through her branches and the mown
And planted garden of her private view.
Those yesterdays no longer *I* but *you.*

Was it her knowledge of the clouded womb
That crowded out her quiet corridors:
Her certainty of child? Or, like far doors

79

Slamming goodbyes, was it a shout of doom,
The dying of a world in her small room:

Her mind a skirt of fear ballooning back
To girlish unencumbered days when life
Required no definitions; sweetheart, wife,
Made love, embroidered, lived without some lack
Of meaning like a rat at every crack:

Mary, still girl enough to twirl her hood
From birth and death conspiring in her blood
Against the bright truth of her platitude?

3

After the dying, tidying her room,
She pondered, wondered why he had cried out
In protest for his father. Was his shout
Indictment of the seed that filled her womb
Or plea for some known name to mark his tomb?
Now she was parched and hollowed out with doubt.

She had been satisfied the way things were,
Girl among girls, doing the usual things.
Then she had been exalted, hearing wings
Applauding through the galleries of air;
Came to know words that first had made her stare,
And talk to common people as to kings.

It never was her doing. She had been
Only the bottle for the conjured wine.
Involved with something magic or divine,
She had no axe to grind, no slate to clean,
Had never bothered with a party line.
Most of the things he said she did not mean.

Now she was empty. The last drop had gone,
And she was her own Mary, uninvolved
With parables or politics, resolved
To self, undedicated, pledged to none.
And just before the colours blurred, dissolved,
She closed the door on her disfigured son.

4

I am the breath that stirred
Your bells to jubilance;
Conjured from cold distance
As surely as a bird
Immense obeisance:
I am the word.

My irresponsible
Dialogue broke down,
Was hooted, hissed and blown
Off stage in ridicule,
My sad forgiving clown
A love-crossed fool.

But I would blow again
My horn into your sleep;
Herd rational thought like sheep
Into a nursery pen;
Scatter my wolves to sweep
Doubt from the plain.

Yes, I would fill your page,
Your lines with poetry:
With liberating key
Empty the clipped lark's cage,
And give back wings to free
Ecstatic rage.

Mary, I am cold,
Bare on the brink of mind.
Open, and let me find
A place to grip and hold,
To thrust the exiled seed
In knowing mould.

FIRST LETTER TO AN IRISH NOVELIST

for Michael McLaverty

Establishment has taken to the hills.
The capitals are bombed. But you pursue
Survival in minute particulars,
Your landscapes, intimate with sea and sky,
Perpetual, unblemished idiom
Common as dolmens and the Easter whin.

Even this city reveals dignity,
Turning a startled face from history.
If you ignore the adolescent dream,
The club-fists of the mob, the tumbled bed,
It is because, the final pattern known,
You choose the threads. And local hatreds fail
To churn your vistas into stony grass,
Or drown you in a puddle's politics.

Chance friendships are not always fortunate.
I think of someone, mutually known,
Complacent as a throstle bosoming song
Above the matchstick silhouetted town
Caught in the headlights of advancing war;
And of another portly pedant who
Talks of the revolution from a chair,

Stroking his stomach; and of that old man
Walking in mountains, gnarled with stern regret
At missing greatness (the erratic bus).

And being Irish means the maudlin song,
A dirty glass, malice, a whispered gibe;
Few to demur when normal decency's
Perverted by a cause or fulsome words,
Uttered by poets and adopted by
Slogan-addicted candidates for power,
Or turned to dogma in schoolchildren's mouths.

Those who have lost a country, with a wound
In place of patria, can sail like winds
Among the islands and the continents,
Flying, if any, only personal flags,
Educated to brave devious seas,
Sceptical of harbours, fortunate
In being themselves, each with his personal war.

And they have charts and compasses, for some
Have made the voyage out before our time,
Confronting tempests, fangs of submarines,
Alerted to the coasts' hostility,
The accents foreign and the flags suspect.
A few received an ocean burial,
Having lost sight of continents too long,
Crazed by a magnitude of space and time,
Agnostic salt in the nostalgic wound.

We shall be wary then, and weatherwise,
Testing our strength of sail, learning the ways
Of sinuous currents singing in the rocks,
And the exotic dreams that come from thirst
And too much loneliness on the world's edge,

The fear of mutiny and the dark hold,
The shark's fin in the wave, the loitering mines.

In time the navigator holds a course,
And heads for landfall. Yes; but, you'll observe,
The missions follow, organised with flags
And bibles for the natives. Be assured
The paths and footholds left by us will fill
With vendors of a new conformity,
Briefed by accountants. Turn to the running sea,
That carries shells like mouths to the hushed sand.

STRINGER'S FIELD

This is no proper route for middle-age
Seeking the stirrups of a rocking horse,
Key lacking door, superior car too big
For the meagre streets of Kick-the-can and Tig.

I have gone back too far. Then a townland,
Before the first death, brimmed and hummed with summer,
And life like loafing kerbstones stretched eternal
And The News was always the same from wireless and
    journal.

I have gone back too far. Then that white summer
Trite with daisies and the next-door girl's
Buttercup kiss through the laurels when we were seven,
And at night the streetlamp guttering up to heaven,

My robining boyhood under Stringer's trees:
Now, leafed back, reveals the kerbstones cold,
Kiss blown, ironic laurels unallayed
By my return to all I left unsaid.

THE GRAND CENTRAL HOTEL

for Robert Greacen

1

    In June, examiners
    Seconded from
The London Guildhall School
Of Music (Speech and Drama) commandeered
    The Londonderry Room,
And summoned elocution-anglicised
Provincials to pout London vowel-sounds;
    Posed as it were
    For kiss or medicine:

    Where, testily carpeted,
    They diffidently
Surrendered up their lines,
Still fighting shy of their stepmother tongue;
    While, down-to-earth, below,
Incorrigibly aboriginal,
The pageboy squired his privileged reserve,
    Between the lift
    And the revolving door.

2

When officers and their whores,
Hotfoot for the hotel,
Forced you back to the gutter's lip,
You reckoned them as war's
Recruitment of the rubbish-tip,
And counted your contempt contemptible;

When, out of character,
You threw off diffidence,

And remonstrated in the street
Against the abattoir,
The flatulent bellow and the bleat
Of butcher's meat dressed up as citizens;

Reluctant activist:
What forced you to declare
Your singlemindedness before
A crowd you still mistrust?
It wasn't love. No; rather more
Distaste, and loyalty, and being there.

3

Then came the palmy days when affluence,
        With cash in hand,
Benevolently knocked at doors,
        A Fyffe-banana man,
Paid to give money to the provident.

Swanning in taxis past the river's sleep,
        Or rakishly
Riding the Jaguar, we lived
        It up, you should observe,
In gracious living as distinct from Life.

Upholstered corners intimate with drink's
        Complicity,
A world in a glimmering glass, to be sipped
        In purchased elegance,
A world away from the world and the shout in the street:

Where dainty legs and unembarrassed eyes,
        The delicate tilt
Of cigarette red from the lips,
        Concealed in masquerade
The idiomatic hatred of their streets.

4

This is hostile territory now.
In Royal Avenue
Planners and bombers have united to
Wreck or eliminate
Taken-for-granted, only-to-be-missed
Familiar presences.
You miss the water when the well runs dry.

Here, where a drunk tycoon
Hoovered the street at midnight, singing psalms,
God's self-appointed broom,
You wore out pavements tracking titles down
To Greer's in Gresham Street;
Over the way, your alter ego read
A wheen of titles too.

Those boarded windows once held waxwork boys
In blazer, cap and tie,
Models of uniform propriety,
Observed on Saturdays
When you descended on the bandying town
With florin or half-crown
Warm as a girl's hand urgent on the thigh.

When, impecunious
Poets, we chose to use the lavatory
Inside the grand hotel,
Disdaining public inconveniences,
We'd sometimes buttonhole
And hold in chat persons of consequence,
As if lounge lizards there.

This hostile territory's symbolised
By the bricked-up hotel

Inside a cage to keep the bombers out,
Where soldiers document
The dirty tricks of violence, and you
From time to time attend
For leave to motor through Victoria Square.

MY MOTHER'S YOUNG SISTER

A new decade, the teacher cried,
Clapping chalk from her hands.
Then: 1930. Someone laughed
Uncertainly; the rest of us were awed.

By 1939 we'd be
Coping with Life, she said.
Did I hold back a thought for you
Trapped in the Twenties, young Persephone?

My youth, not yours, is stirred again
By summer photographs,
Items of Twentyish furniture,
That outfaced decades you have never known.

But, in sleep's undertone, you came,
Sidestepping memory,
Vivid, vivacious; unperturbed
By futures come and gone after your time.

And I caught at your perfume, and
Half-heard the teacher say
You are a shade too old for him:
Above my head, as though you'd understand.

But such discrepancy in years
Death stands upon its head:
You, twenty-three for ever now,
My age careering towards my grandfather's.

You were a girl who hurried past
My childhood, with a dream's
Inconstancy; as if forewarned,
Time being short, you had to travel fast.

FOR THE RECORD

Herbertson telephoned:
In need of someone old enough, he said,
To put back into context incidents
That happened in our time,
Which hearsay garbles and misrepresents.

A sharp American
Cocked his recorder for the interview;
Unloaded questions. *You and I were there*,
I mocked; and Herbertson
Sagely concurred, and trimmed his smouldering briar.

Identity; degree
Of Irishness; the label on the jar,
Backed by his books, the old man underlined
I am of Planter stock.
A ring of smoke endorsed his nodding hand.

Planter and Gael. Estranged
From both the new grim Irish and the old
Colonial retrospection, I held forth
Over the scurrying tape.
When I was a barefoot lad in the English North.

PADRAIC FIACC

b. 1924

GLOSS

Nor truth nor good did they know
But beauty burning away.

They were the dark earth people
                              of old
Restive in the clay . . .

Deirdre watched Naisi die
And great King Conor of himself
                              said

'Did you ever see a bottomless
                    bucket
In the muck discarded?'

And comradely Dermot was destroyed by Fionn

Because of the beauty of a girl.

Because of the beauty of a girl
The sky went raging on fire

And the sea was pushed out into
                              rage.

They were the dark earth people
                              of old

And Deirdre pitched herself into
                              the sea.

Turn the page. Turn the page.

FIRST MOVEMENT

for Alan Rodgers

Low clouds yellow in a mist wind
Sift on far-off ards
Drift hazily . . .

I was born on such a morning
Smelling of the Bone Yards

The smoking chimneys over
                    the slate roof tops
The wayward storm birds

And to the east where morning is
                              the sea
And to the west where evening is
                              the sea
Threatening with danger
                         and it
Would always darken suddenly.

SOLDIERS

for Seamus Deane

The altar boy marches up the altar steps.
The priest marches down. 'Get up now
And be a soldier!' says the nun
To the woman after giving birth, 'Get up now
And march, march: Be a man!'

And the men are men and the women are men
And the children are men!

Mother carried a knife to work.
It was the thorn to her rose . . .

They say she died with her eyes open
In the French Hospital in New York.
I remember those eyes shining in the dark

Slum hallway the day after
I left the monastery: Eyes that were
A feast of welcome that said 'Yes,
I'm glad you didn't stay stuck there!'

'Would you mind if I went to prison
Rather than war?'
'No, for Ireland's men all went to prison!'

At the bottom of a canyon of brick
She cursed and swore
'You never see the sky!'

A lifetime after
                    just before
I go to sleep at night, I hear

That Anna Magnani voice screaming
Me deaf 'No! No, you're not
To heed the world!' In one swift
Sentence she tells me not to yield
But to *forbear:*

                'Go to prison but never
Never stop fighting. We are the poor
And the poor have to be "soldiers".

'You're still a soldier, it's only that
You're losing the war

'And all the wars are lost anyway!'

THE BRITISH CONNECTION

A litany of terror

In Belfast, Europe, your man
Met the Military come to raid
The house: 'Over my dead body
Sir,' he said, brandishing
A real-life sword from some
Old half-forgotten war . . .

And youths with real bows and arrows
And coppers and marbles good as bullets
And old time thrupenny bits and stones,
Screws, bolts, nuts (Belfast confetti),

And kitchen knives, pokers, Guinness tins
And nail-bombs down by the Shore Road

And guns under the harbour wharf
And bullets in the docker's tea tin

And gelignite in the tool shed
And grenades in the scullery larder
And weedkiller and sugar
And acid in the French letter

And sodium chlorate and nitrates
In the suburban garage
In the boot of the car

And guns in the oven grill
And guns in the spinster's shift

And ammunition and more, more
Guns in the broken-down rusted
Merry-go-round in the scrapyard –

Almost as many hard-on
Guns as there are Union Jacks.

ENEMY ENCOUNTER

for Lilac

Dumping (left over from the autumn)
Dead leaves, near a culvert
I come on
                a British Army Soldier
With a rifle and a radio
Perched hiding. He has red hair.

He is young enough to be my weenie
-bopper daughter's boyfriend.
He is like a lonely little winter robin.

We are that close to each other, I
Can nearly hear his heart beating.

I say something bland to make him grin,
But his glass eyes look past my side
-whiskers down
                    the Shore Road street.
I am an Irish man
                    and he is afraid
That I have come to kill him.

INTIMATE LETTER 1973

Our Paris part of Belfast has
Decapitated lamp-posts now. Our meeting
Place, the Book Shop, is a gaping
Black hole of charred timber.

Remember that night with you, in-
valided in the top room when
They were throwing petrol bombs through
The windows of Catholics, how
My migraine grew to such
A pitch, Brigid said 'Mommy,
I think Daddy is going to burst!'

We all run away from each other's
Particular hell. I didn't
Survive you and her thrown
To the floor when they blew up the Co-
Op at the bottom of the street or Brigid
Waking screaming after this

Or that explosion. Really,
I was the first one to go:

It was I who left you . . .

SAINT COLEMAN'S SONG FOR FLIGHT/
  AN *ITE MISSA EST*

for Nancy and Brigid – flown

Run like rats from the plague in you.
Before death it is no virtue to be dead.
The crannog in the water, anywhere at all sure!
It is no virtue and it is not nature
To wait to writhe into the ground.

Not one in the Bible could see these dead
Packed on top of the other like dung
Not the two Josephs in Egypt
But would not run!

And Christ's blessing follow
(Is it not a blessing to escape storm?)

Pray to old Joseph – not a witless man –
Who had the brains not to want to die

But when his time came only and at home in bed,
The door shut on the world, that wolf outside
Munching the leper's head.

JOHN MONTAGUE

b. 1929

LIKE DOLMENS ROUND MY CHILDHOOD, THE OLD PEOPLE

Like dolmens round my childhood, the old people.

Jamie MacCrystal sang to himself
A broken song, without tune, without words;
He tipped me a penny every pension day,
Fed kindly crusts to winter birds.
When he died his cottage was robbed,
Mattress and money box torn and searched,
Only the corpse they didn't disturb.

Maggie Owens was surrounded by animals,
A mongrel bitch and shivering pups,
Even in her bedroom a she-goat cried,
She was a well of gossip defiled,
Fanged chronicler of a whole countryside;
Reputed a witch, all I could find
Was her lonely need to deride.

The Nialls lived along a mountain lane
Where heather bells bloomed, clumps of foxglove.
All were blind, with Blind Pension and Wireless.
Dead eyes serpent-flickered as one entered
To shelter from a downpour of mountain rain.
Crickets chirped under the rocking hearthstone
Until the muddy sun shone out again.

Mary Moore lived in a crumbling gatehouse
Famous as Pisa for its leaning gable.
Bag apron and boots, she tramped the fields

Driving lean cattle to a miry stable.
A byword for fierceness, she fell asleep
Over love stories, Red Star and Red Circle,
Dreamed of gypsy love rites, by firelight sealed.

Wild Billy Eagleson married a Catholic servant girl
When all his loyal family passed on:
We danced round him shouting 'To hell with King Billy'
And dodged from the arc of his flailing blackthorn.
Forsaken by both creeds, he showed little concern
Until the Orange drums banged past in the summer
And bowler and sash aggressively shone.

Curate and doctor trudged to attend them,
Through knee-deep snow, through summer heat,
From main road to lane to broken path,
Gulping the mountain air with painful breath.
Sometimes they were found by neighbours,
Silent keepers of a smokeless hearth,
Suddenly cast in the mould of death.

Ancient Ireland, indeed! I was reared by her bedside,
The rune and the chant, evil eye and averted head,
Fomorian fierceness of family and local feud.
Gaunt figures of fear and of friendliness,
For years they trespassed on my dreams,
Until once, in a standing circle of stones,
I felt their shadows pass

Into that dark permanence of ancient forms.

THE CAGE

My father, the least happy
man I have known. His face

98

retained the pallor
of those who work underground:
the lost years in Brooklyn
listening to a subway
shudder the earth.

But a traditional Irishman
who (released from his grille
in the Clark St IRT)
drank neat whiskey until
he reached the only element
he felt at home in
any longer: brute oblivion.

And yet picked himself
up, most mornings,
to march down the street
extending his smile
to all sides of the good
(non-negro) neighbourhood
belled by St Teresa's church.

When he came back
we walked together
across fields of Garvaghey
to see hawthorn on the summer
hedges, as though
he had never left;
a bend of the road

which still sheltered
primroses. But we
did not smile in
the shared complicity
of a dream, for when

weary Odysseus returns
Telemachus must leave.

Often as I descend
into subway or underground
I see his bald head behind
the bars of the small booth;
the mark of an old car
accident beating on his
ghostly forehead.

A DRINK OF MILK

In the girdered dark
of the byre, cattle move;
warm engines hushed
to a siding groove

before the switch flicks
down for milking.
In concrete partitions
they rattle their chains

while the farmhand eases
rubber tentacles to tug
lightly but rhythmically
on their swollen dugs

and up the pale cylinders
of the milking machine
mounts an untouched
steadily pulsing stream.

Only the tabby steals
to dip its radar whiskers
with old-fashioned relish
in a chipped saucer

and before Seán lurches
to kick his boots off
in the night-silent kitchen
he draws a mug of froth

to settle on the sideboard
under the hoard of delph.
A pounding transistor shakes
the Virgin on her shelf

as he dreams towards bed.
A last glance at a magazine,
he puts the mug to his head,
grunts, and drains it clean.

A WELCOMING PARTY

Wie war das möglich?

That final newsreel of the war:
A welcoming party of almost shades
Met us at the cinema door
Clicking what remained of their heels.

From nests of bodies like hatching eggs
Flickered insectlike hands and legs
And rose an ululation, terrible, shy;
Children conjugating the verb 'to die'.

One clamoured mutely of love
From a mouth like a burnt glove;
Others upheld hands bleak as begging bowls
Claiming the small change of our souls.

Some smiled at us as protectors.
Can these bones live?
Our parochial brand of innocence
Was all we had to give.

To be always at the periphery of incident
Gave my childhood its Irish dimension; drama of unevent:
Yet doves of mercy, as doves of air,
Can falter here as anywhere.

That long dead Sunday in Armagh
I learned one meaning of total war
And went home to my Christian school
To kick a football through the air.

THE TROUT

Flat on the bank I parted
Rushes to ease my hands
In the water without a ripple
And tilt them slowly downstream
To where he lay, tendril light,
In his fluid sensual dream.

Bodiless lord of creation
I hung briefly above him
Savouring my own absence
Senses expanding in the slow

Motion, the photographic calm
That grows before action.

As the curve of my hands
Swung under his body
He surged, with visible pleasure.
I was so preternaturally close
I could count every stipple
But still cast no shadow, until

The two palms crossed in a cage
Under the lightly pulsing gills.
Then (entering my own enlarged
Shape, which rode on the water)
I gripped. To this day I can
Taste his terror in my hands.

ALL LEGENDARY OBSTACLES

All legendary obstacles lay between
Us, the long imaginary plain,
The monstrous ruck of mountains
And, swinging across the night,
Flooding the Sacramento, San Joaquin,
The hissing drift of winter rain.

All day I waited, shifting
Nervously from station to bar
As I saw another train sail
By, the San Francisco Chief or
Golden Gate, water dripping
From great flanged wheels.

At midnight you came, pale
Above the negro porter's lamp.
I was too blind with rain
And doubt to speak, but
Reached from the platform
Until our chilled hands met.

You had been travelling for days
With an old lady, who marked
A neat circle on the glass
With her glove, to watch us
Move into the wet darkness
Kissing, still unable to speak.

THE SAME GESTURE

There is a secret room
of golden light where
everything – love, violence,
hatred is possible;
and, again love.

Such intimacy of hand
and mind is achieved
under its healing light
that the shifting of
hands is a rite

like court music.
We barely know our
selves there though
it is what we always were
– most nakedly are –

and must remember
when we leave, re-
suming our habits
with our clothes:
work, phone, drive

through late traffic
changing gears with
the same gesture as
eased your snowbound
heart and flesh.

HERBERT STREET REVISITED

for Madeleine

I

A light is burning late
in this Georgian Dublin street:
someone is leading our old lives!

And our black cat scampers again
through the wet grass of the convent garden
upon his masculine errands.

The pubs shut: a released bull,
Behan shoulders up the street,
topples into our basement, roaring 'John!'

A pony and donkey cropped flank
by flank under the trees opposite;
short neck up, long neck down,

as Nurse Mullen knelt by her bedside
to pray for her lost Mayo hills,
the bruised bodies of Easter Volunteers.

Animals, neighbours, treading the pattern
of one time and place into history,
like our early marriage, while

tall windows looked down upon us
from walls flushed light pink or salmon
watching and enduring succession.

II

As I leave, you whisper,
'don't betray our truth'
and like a ghost dancer,
invoking a lost tribal strength
I halt in tree-fed darkness

to summon back our past,
and celebrate a love that eased
so kindly, the dying bone,
enabling the spirit to sing
of old happiness, when alone.

III

So put the leaves back on the tree,
put the tree back in the ground,
let Brendan trundle his corpse down
the street singing, like Molly Malone.

Let the black cat, tiny emissary
of our happiness, streak again
through the darkness, to fall soft
clawed into a landlord's dustbin.

Let Nurse Mullen take the last
train to Westport, and die upright
in her chair, facing a window
warm with the blue slopes of Nephin.

And let the pony and donkey come –
look, someone has left the gate open –
like hobbyhorses linked in
the slow motion of a dream

parading side by side, down
the length of Herbert Street,
rising and falling, lifting
their hooves through the moonlight.

THE POINT

Rocks jagged in morning mist.
At intervals, the foghorn sounds
From the white lighthouse rock
Lonely as cow mourning her calf,
Groaning, belly deep, desperate.

I assisted at such failure once;
A night-long fight to save a calf
Born finally, with broken neck.
It flailed briefly on the straw,
A wide-eyed mother straddling it.

Listen carefully. This is different.
It sounds to guide, not lament.
When the defining light is powerless,
Ships hesitating down the strait
Hear its harsh voice as friendliness.

Upstairs my wife and daughter sleep.
Our two lives have separated now
But I would send my voice to yours
Cutting through the shrouding mist
Like some friendly signal in distress.

The fog is lifting, slowly.
Flag high, a new ship is entering.
The opposite shore unveils itself
Bright in detail as a painting,
Alone, but equal to the morning.

WINDHARP

for Patrick Collins

The sounds of Ireland,
that restless whispering
you never get away
from, seeping out of
low bushes and grass,
heatherbells and fern,
wrinkling bog pools,
scraping tree branches,
light hunting cloud,
sound hounding sight,
a hand ceaselessly
combing and stroking
the landscape, till
the valley gleams
like the pile upon
a mountain pony's coat.

THE SILVER FLASK

Sweet, though short, our
hours as a family together.
Driving across dark mountains
to Midnight Mass in Fivemiletown,
lights coming up in the valleys
as in the days of Carleton.

Tussocks of heather brown
in the headlights; our mother
stowed in the back, a tartan
rug wrapped round her knees,
patiently listening as Father sang,
and the silver flask went round.

Chorus after chorus of the *Adoremus*
to shorten the road before us,
till *we see amidst the winter's snows*
the festive lights of the small town
and from the choirloft an organ booms
angels we have heard on high, with

my father joining warmly in,
his broken tenor soaring, faltering,
a legend in dim bars of Brooklyn
(that sacramental moment of stillness
among exiled, disgruntled men)
now raised vehemently once again

in the valleys he had sprung from,
startling the stiff congregation
with fierce blasts of song, while
our mother sat silent beside him,
sad but proud, an unaccustomed
blush mantling her wan countenance.

Then driving slowly home,
tongues crossed with the communion
wafer, snowflakes melting in
the car's hungry headlights,
till we reach the warm kitchen
and the spirits round again.

The family circle briefly restored
nearly twenty lonely years after
that last Christmas in Brooklyn,
under the same tinsel of decorations
so carefully hoarded by our mother
in the cabin trunk of a Cunard liner.

LAST JOURNEY

I.M. James Montague

We stand together
on the windy platform;
how crisp the rails
running out of sight
through the wet fields!

Carney, the station master,
is peering over
his frosted window:
the hand of the signal
points down.

Crowned with churns
a cart creaks up the
incline of Main Street
to the sliding doors
of the Co-op.

A smell of coal,
the train is coming . . .
you climb slowly in,
propped by my hand to
a seat, back to the engine,

and we leave, waving
a plume of black smoke
over the rushy meadows,
small hills & hidden villages –
Beragh, Carrickmore,

Pomeroy, Fintona –
place names that sigh
like a pressed melodeon
across this forgotten
Northern landscape.

HEARTH SONG

for Seamus Heaney

1

The Nialls' cottage had one:
it lived under a large flagstone,
loving the warmth of the kitchen.

Chill or silent, for whole days,
it would, all of a sudden, start
its constant, compelling praise.

And all of us, dreaming or chatting
over the fire, would go quiet,
harkening to that insistent creak,

Accustoming ourselves all over again
to that old, but always strange sound
coming at us from under the ground,

Rising from beneath our feet,
welling up out of the earth,
a solitary, compulsive song

Composed for no one, a tune
dreamt up under a flat stone,
earth's fragile, atonal rhythm.

2

And did I once glimpse one?
I call up that empty farmhouse,
its blind, ghostly audience

And a boy's bare legs dangling
down from a stool, as he peers
through a crack in the flagstones

And here it strikes up again,
that minute, manic cellist,
scraping the shape of itself,

Its shining, blue-black back
and pulsing, tendril limbs
throbbing and trembling in darkness

a hearth song of happiness.

JAMES SIMMONS

b. 1933

THE INFLUENCE OF NATURAL OBJECTS

for Bill Ireland

Night after night from our camp on Sugar Loaf Hill
We strolled the streets, roaring or quiet, daring
Anything for girls or drink, but not caring
When the town closed. We reeled home and were ill,
Cooked fries, fell senseless in our socks
On grass or blankets. I woke cold at dawn
And stumbled to the Hill Top Zoo, and on
Through pines to the bare summit's litter of rocks.
I was always scared by the huge spaces below,
Between sky and water, explosive bright air
Glinting on live-wire nerves of mine, worn bare.
I lay down, grinning, stiff with vertigo.

This roused an appetite for breakfast, bars,
Bathing, chasing the daft holiday bitches,
For jokes and poems, beer and sandwiches . . .
And so on till we slept under the stars.

STEPHANO REMEMBERS

We broke out of our dream into a clearing
and there were all our masters still sneering.
My head bowed, I made jokes and turned away,
living over and over that strange day.

The ship struck before morning. Half-past four,
on a huge hogshead of claret I swept ashore

like an evangelist aboard his god:
his will was mine, I laughed and kissed the rod,
and would have walked that foreign countryside
blind drunk, contentedly, till my god died;
but finding Trinculo made it a holiday:
two Neapolitans had got away,
and that shipload of scheming toffs we hated
was drowned. Never to be humiliated
again, 'I will no more to sea,' I sang.
Down white empty beaches my voice rang,
and that dear monster, half-fish and half-man,
went on his knees to me. Oh, Caliban,
you thought I'd take your twisted master's life;
but a drunk butler's slower with a knife
than your fine courtiers, your dukes, your kings.
We were distracted by too many things . . .
the wine, the jokes, the music, fancy gowns.
We were no good as murderers, we were clowns.

LULLABY FOR RACHAEL

All your days are holy days,
in dreams begins your terror.
Predetermined are the ways
perfection comes to error.

Flaws, like hands used in the sun,
will gradually harden.
You, as your elders did, will run
from simple things, from the garden.

Sleeping when each day is through,
practise for your death.

Learn each law you're subject to
within your lease of breath.

My world is mapped imperfectly:
here I once found treasure,
friends here, here the enemy;
alter it with pleasure.

Changing the boundary lines, I fear,
has made my map a mess.
By seeing more you may draw clear,
but not by seeing less.

The lullaby was adequate,
you'll sleep until the morning.
How little we communicate,
how useless is this warning.

Though I have failed to make you wise
with all the words above,
I've made, while trying to tell no lies,
a noise to go with love.

JOIN ME IN CELEBRATING

Join me in celebrating
This unhoped-for gift
She has brought me sweating
In a crumpled shift.
Pushed through my wife,
My letter box, appears
A present of life,
Bald head and flattened ears,

Parcelled in blood and slime,
A loosely wrapped thing
Unlabelled but on time,
String dangling.
I wouldn't change my condition
For freedom, cash, applause,
Rebirth of young ambition
Or faith in Santa Claus.

A BIRTHDAY POEM

for Rachael

For every year of life we light
a candle on your cake
to mark the simple sort of progress
anyone can make,
and then, to test your nerve or give
a proper view of death,
you're asked to blow each light, each year,
out with your own breath.

ONE OF THE BOYS

Our youth was gay but rough,
much drink and copulation.
If that seems not enough
blame our miseducation.
In shabby boarding houses
lips covered lips,
and in our wild carouses
there were companionships.

Cheap and mundane the setting
of all that we remember:
in August, dance-hall petting,
cinemas in December.
Now middle-aged I know,
and do not hide the truth,
used or misused years go
and take all kinds of youth.
We test the foreign scene
or grow too fat in banks,
salesmen for margarine,
soldiers in tanks,
the great careers all tricks,
the fine arts all my arse,
business and politics
a cruel farce.
Though fear of getting fired
may ease, and work is hated
less, we are tired, tired
and incapacitated.
On golf courses, in bars,
crutched by the cash we earn,
we think of nights in cars
with energy to burn.

DIDN'T HE RAMBLE

for Michael Longley

'The family wanted to make a bricklayer of him, but Ferd. was
too smooth and clever a fellow. He preferred to sit in the parlour
out of the sun and play piano.'

Henry Morton

There was a hardware shop in Main Street sold
records as well as spades and plastic bowls.
Jo, the assistant, had a taste for jazz.

117

The shop being empty as it mostly was
I tried out records, then, like seeing the light,
but genuine, I heard Josh White:
I'M GOING TO MO-O-VE YOU, WAY ON THE OUTSKIRTS OF TOWN.
Where was my turntable to set it down!
A voice styled by experience, learning to make
music listening to Blind Willie Blake,
walking the streets of a city, avoiding cops,
toting a cheap guitar and begging box.

The campus poets used to write of saxophones
disgustedly and sneer at gramophones;
but the word of life, if such a thing existed,
was there on record among the rubbish listed
in the catalogues of Brunswick and HMV,
healing the split in sensibility.
Tough reasonableness and lyric grace
together, in poor man's dialect.
Something that no one taught us to expect.
Profundity without the po-face
of court and bourgeois modes. This I could use
to live and die with. Jazz. Blues.
I love the music and the men who made
the music, and instruments they played:
saxophone, piano, trumpet, clarinet,
Bill Broonzy, Armstrong, Basie, Hodges, Chet
Baker, Garner, Tommy Ladnier,
Jelly Roll Morton, Bessie Smith, Bechet,
and Fats Waller, the scholar–clown of song
who sang 'Until the Real Thing Comes Along'.
Here was the risen people, their feet
dancing, not out to murder the elite:
'Pardon me, sir, may we be free?
The kitchen staff is having a jamboree.'

History records how people cleared the shelves
of record shops, discovering themselves,
making distinctions in the ordinary,
seeing what they'd been too tired to see;
but most ignored the music. Some were scared,
some greedy, some condemned what they hadn't heard,
some sold cheap imitations, watered it down,
bribed Fats to drink too much and play the clown
instead of the piano, and failed – the man was wise,
he did both painlessly. Jazz is a compromise:
you take the first tune in your head and play
until it's saying what you want to say.
'I ain't got no diplomas,' said Satchmo,
'I look into my heart and blow.'

What if some great ones took to drugs and drink
and killed themselves? Only a boy could think
the world cures easy, and want to blame
someone. I know I'll never be the same.
A mad world, my masters! We might have known
that Wardell Gray was only well spoken,
controlled and elegant on saxophone.
He appeared last in a field with his neck broken.
The jazz life did it, not the Ku Klux Klan.
Whatever made the music killed the man.

EDEN

He threw them out and slammed the gate shut
for what He found them up to. He was scared
like all angry people and unprepared
for love. He decided to blame it on 'that slut'.

Morally hungover He walked the walls,
straightened His stone picnic tables, stared
sickly at the new padlock and the guard's sword,
waiting to welcome repentant prodigals.

If only they'd argue, face to face; but no.
They sneaked back to pick up a radio
left in a secret place in the undergrowth,
aimlessness their element they were loath
to risk losing. They drifted into the night,
relieved in every way to travel light.
The unprejudiced world was what those two lacked,
and of course they avoided the huge pathetic back
of God. To this day He is standing there,
banished. There *was* a world elsewhere.

AFTER EDEN

His last glimpse of the former wife
is after midnight, woozy with drink,
on a quick foray for old tapes,
and the front door is open, as always,
out of their shared instinct.

A ghost in his own shadowy hall,
the stairwell echoing still
with bitter shouting and slammed doors,
up in his old study he opens drawers,
and descends, his thieving arms full.

A man comes out of the kitchen and disappears.
At the car the wife grabs him, hissing abuse.
Hunched awkwardly, unloading his loot,

his high-pitched voice whining, 'Christ
you've got everything else!' – he breaks loose,

'Look! We agreed . . .' 'I agreed to nothing!
It was YOU walked out on ME with your whore!'
When he hits her, precious tapes unreel
and roll on the pavement. Again they are sharing
intimate touch – her nose, his knuckles, sore.

Will the long marriage never be over?
Love she would call what drives her now to close
fiercely against him, drinking his anger,
shameless and righteous, fronting
her husband, embracing his futile blows.

His last glimpse is of her standing
in faded chiffon nightwear, humble, beautiful,
like a dark harvest etching, 'The Last Gleaner',
a woman, lit by a streetlamp, winding
tangles of gleaming tape on a plastic spool.

FOR IMELDA

There were no poems that year,
but every night driving from work
the red haws on the hedges
took me unawares, looming
in the milky car beams
as lush as cherries;
a sign they said of the hard
winter to come or maybe
the loveliest summer
in living memory,
my memory, my dear.

THE HONEYMOON

Remember last summer when God turned on the heat
and browned our bodies, remember how hard and sweet
were the green apples you bought.
Remember how quickly neglected nipples were taught
to take pleasure in kissing. Remember your sunburn peeled
after a day on the grass of the hill field
and the painless scars evoked a principle for us,
that the truly lovely is truly ridiculous.

A beauty like you can look sometimes dumpy and fat,
knock-kneed, hen-toed, and none the worse for that,
for when you recover your splendour suddenly
what seemed like flaws is personality.
The world has examined you closely and found you right
and beautiful with a more piercing sight
than fashion editors know. You thought I meant
evasion, a left-handed compliment;
but now know better, being able to talk to you
like this is love being true.

Nothing could get us down those days together
but lust, on grass, in mountain streams when the weather
was hot as ourselves, on collapsing sofas, on floors,
in the steamed-up Datsun in the great outdoors.
Our best man swore you would be black and blue,
and, true enough, love's frightening. You do
violent-seeming things; but no one's hurt,
playing by the rules. We rise from dirt,
stink, struggle, shining, having suffered nothing.
No wonder they say that God would have us loving.

The worst débâcle was, once, trying to screw,
erect, me knees-bent, on my feet, and you

tiptoe on Dickens's *Our Mutual Friend*.
No joy. Abashed, we thought it was the end
of something; but no, failing is all right,
a sort of roughage to the appetite.

Our strangest luck seemed, first, not good, but ill –
me slow to come, you inexhaustible.
That turned out well. I had not thought God's voice
was intricate and humorous, like Joyce's.

Even your tears, after our first quarrel
when you got strangely thick and I got moral,
were not exploitive. Remember our briny kiss?
Nothing was broken, nothing was amiss.

FROM THE IRISH

Most terrible was our hero in battle blows:
hands without fingers, shorn heads and toes
were scattered. That day there flew and fell
from astonished victims eyebrow, bone and entrail,
like stars in the sky, like snowflakes, like nuts in May,
like a meadow of daisies, like butts from an ashtray.

Familiar things, you might brush against or tread
upon in the daily round, were glistening red
with the slaughter the hero caused, though he had gone.
By proxy his bomb exploded, his valour shone.

SEAMUS HEANEY

b. 1939

FOLLOWER

My father worked with a horse-plough,
His shoulders globed like a full sail strung
Between the shafts and the furrow.
The horses strained at his clicking tongue.

An expert. He would set the wing
And fit the bright steel-pointed sock.
The sod rolled over without breaking.
At the headrig, with a single pluck

Of reins, the sweating team turned round
And back into the land. His eye
Narrowed and angled at the ground,
Mapping the furrow exactly.

I stumbled in his hobnailed wake,
Fell sometimes on the polished sod;
Sometimes he rode me on his back
Dipping and rising to his plod.

I wanted to grow up and plough,
To close one eye, stiffen my arm.
All I ever did was follow
In his broad shadow round the farm.

I was a nuisance, tripping, falling,
Yapping always. But today
It is my father who keeps stumbling
Behind me, and will not go away.

BOGLAND

for T.P. Flanagan

We have no prairies
To slice a big sun at evening –
Everywhere the eye concedes to
Encroaching horizon,

Is wooed into the cyclops' eye
Of a tarn. Our unfenced country
Is bog that keeps crusting
Between the sights of the sun.

They've taken the skeleton
Of the Great Irish Elk
Out of the peat, set it up
An astounding crate full of air.

Butter sunk under
More than a hundred years
Was recovered salty and white.
The ground itself is kind, black butter

Melting and opening underfoot,
Missing its last definition
By millions of years.
They'll never dig coal here,

Only the waterlogged trunks
Of great firs, soft as pulp.
Our pioneers keep striking
Inwards and downwards,

Every layer they strip
Seems camped on before.

The bogholes might be Atlantic seepage.
The wet centre is bottomless.

THE TOLLUND MAN

1

Some day I will go to Aarhus
To see his peat-brown head,
The mild pods of his eyelids,
His pointed skin cap.

In the flat country nearby
Where they dug him out,
His last gruel of winter seeds
Caked in his stomach,

Naked except for
The cap, noose and girdle,
I will stand a long time.
Bridegroom to the goddess,

She tightened her torc on him
And opened her fen,
Those dark juices working
Him to a saint's kept body,

Trove of the turfcutters'
Honeycombed workings.
Now his stained face
Reposes at Aarhus.

2

I could risk blasphemy,
Consecrate the cauldron bog
Our holy ground and pray
Him to make germinate

The scattered, ambushed
Flesh of labourers,
Stockinged corpses
Laid out in the farmyards,

Telltale skin and teeth
Flecking the sleepers
Of four young brothers, trailed
For miles along the lines.

3

Something of his sad freedom
As he rode the tumbril
Should come to me, driving,
Saying the names

Tollund, Grabaulle, Nebelgard,
Watching the pointing hands
Of country people,
Not knowing their tongue.

Out there in Jutland
In the old man-killing parishes
I will feel lost,
Unhappy and at home.

THE OTHER SIDE

I

Thigh-deep in sedge and marigolds
a neighbour laid his shadow
on the stream, vouching

'It's poor as Lazarus, that ground',
and brushed away
among the shaken leafage:

I lay where his lea sloped
to meet our fallow,
nested on moss and rushes,

my ear swallowing
his fabulous, biblical dismissal,
that tongue of chosen people.

When he would stand like that
on the other side, white-haired,
swinging his blackthorn

at the marsh weeds,
he prophesied above our scraggy acres,
then turned away

towards his promised furrows
on the hill, a wake of pollen
drifting to our bank, next season's tares.

II

For days we would rehearse
each patriarchal dictum:
Lazarus, the Pharaoh, Solomon

and David and Goliath rolled
magnificently, like loads of hay
too big for our small lanes,

or faltered on a rut –
'Your side of the house, I believe,
hardly rule by the book at all.'

His brain was a whitewashed kitchen
hung with texts, swept tidy
as the body o' the kirk.

III

Then sometimes when the rosary was dragging
mournfully on in the kitchen
we would hear his step round the gable

though not until after the litany
would the knock come to the door
and the casual whistle strike up

on the doorstep, 'A right-looking night,'
he might say, 'I was dandering by
and says I, I might as well call.'

But now I stand behind him
in the dark yard, in the moan of prayers.
He puts a hand in a pocket

or taps a little tune with the blackthorn
shyly, as if he were party to
lovemaking or a stranger's weeping.

Should I slip away, I wonder,
or go up and touch his shoulder
and talk about the weather

or the price of grass-seed?

MOSSBAWN: TWO POEMS IN DEDICATION

for Mary Heaney

1   Sunlight

There was a sunlit absence.
The helmeted pump in the yard
heated its iron,
water honeyed

in the slung bucket
and the sun stood
like a griddle cooling
against the wall

of each long afternoon.
So, her hands scuffled
over the bakeboard,
the reddening stove

sent its plaque of heat
against her where she stood
in a floury apron
by the window.

Now she dusts the board
with a goose's wing,

now sits, broad-lapped,
with whitened nails

and measling shins:
here is a space
again, the scone rising
to the tick of two clocks.

And here is love
like a tinsmith's scoop
sunk past its gleam
in the meal-bin.

2   The seed cutters

They seem hundreds of years away. Breughel,
You'll know them if I can get them true.
They kneel under the hedge in a half-circle
Behind a windbreak wind is breaking through.
They are the seed cutters. The tuck and frill
Of leaf-sprout is on the seed potatoes
Buried under that straw. With time to kill
They are taking their time. Each sharp knife goes
Lazily halving each root that falls apart
In the palm of the hand: a milky gleam,
And, at the centre, a dark watermark.
O calendar customs! Under the broom
Yellowing over them, compose the frieze
With all of us there, our anonymities.

EXPOSURE

It is December in Wicklow:
Alders dripping, birches

Inheriting the last light,
The ash tree cold to look at.

A comet that was lost
Should be visible at sunset,
Those million tons of light
Like a glimmer of haws and rosehips,

And I sometimes see a falling star.
If I could come on meteorite!
Instead I walk through damp leaves,
Husks, the spent flukes of autumn,

Imagining a hero
On some muddy compound,
His gift like a slingstone
Whirled for the desperate.

How did I end up like this?
I often think of my friends'
Beautiful prismatic counselling
And the anvil brains of some who hate me

As I sit weighing and weighing
My responsible *tristia*.
For what? For the ear? For the people?
For what is said behind backs?

Rain comes down through the alders,
Its low conducive voices
Mutter about let-downs and erosions
And yet each drop recalls

The diamond absolutes.
I am neither internee nor informer;

An inner émigré, grown long-haired
And thoughtful; a wood-kerne

Escaped from the massacre,
Taking protective colouring
From bole and bark, feeling
Every wind that blows;

Who, blowing up these sparks
For their meagre heat, have missed
The once-in-a-lifetime portent,
The comet's pulsing rose.

THE OTTER

When you plunged
The light of Tuscany wavered
And swung through the pool
From top to bottom.

I loved your wet head and smashing crawl,
Your fine swimmer's back and shoulders
Surfacing and surfacing again
This year and every year since.

I sat dry-throated on the warm stones.
You were beyond me.
The mellowed clarities, the grape-deep air
Thinned and disappointed.

Thank God for the slow loadening,
When I hold you now
We are close and deep
As the atmosphere on water.

My two hands are plumbed water.
You are my palpable, lithe
Otter of memory
In the pool of the moment,

Turning to swim on your back,
Each silent, thigh-shaking kick
Re-tilting the light,
Heaving the cool at your neck.

And suddenly you're out,
Back again, intent as ever,
Heavy and frisky in your freshened pelt,
Printing the stones.

A POSTCARD FROM NORTH ANTRIM

in memory of Sean Armstrong

A lone figure is waving
From the thin line of a bridge
Of ropes and slats, slung
Dangerously out between
The cliff-top and the pillar rock.
A nineteenth-century wind.
Dulse-pickers. Sea campions.

A postcard for you, Sean,
And that's you, swinging alone,
Antic, half-afraid,
In your gallowglass's beard
And swallow-tail of serge:
The Carrick-a-Rede Rope Bridge
Ghost-written on sepia.

134

Or should it be your houseboat
Ethnically furnished,
Redolent of grass?
Should we discover you
Beside those warm-planked, democratic wharves
Among the twilights and guitars
Of Sausalito?

Dropout on a comeback,
Prince of no-man's-land
With your head in clouds or sand,
You were the clown
Social worker of the town
Until your candid forehead stopped
A pointblank teatime bullet.

Get up from your blood on the floor.
Here's another boat
In grass by the lough shore,
Turf smoke, a wired hen-run –
Your local, hoped for, unfound commune.
Now recite me *William Bloat*,
Sing of the *Calabar*

Or of Henry Joy McCracken
Who kissed his Mary Ann
On the gallows at Cornmarket.
Or Ballycastle Fair.
'Give us the raw bar!'
'Sing it by brute force
If you forget the air.'

Yet something in your voice
Stayed nearly shut.
Your voice was a harassed pulpit

Leading the melody
It kept at bay,
It was independent, rattling, non-transcendent
Ulster – old decency

And Old Bushmills,
Soda farls, strong tea,
New rope, rock salt, kale plants,
Potato bread and Woodbine.
Wind through the concrete vents
Of a border checkpoint.
Cold zinc nailed for a peace line.

Fifteen years ago, come this October,
Crowded on your floor,
I got my arm round Marie's shoulder
For the first time.
'Oh, Sir Jasper, do not touch me!'
You roared across at me,
Chorus-leading, splashing out the wine.

THE HARVEST BOW

As you plaited the harvest bow
You implicated the mellowed silence in you
In wheat that does not rust
But brightens as it tightens twist by twist
Into a knowable corona,
A throwaway love knot of straw.

Hands that aged round ashplants and cane sticks
And lapped the spurs on a lifetime of game cocks
Harked to their gift and worked with fine intent

Until your fingers moved somnambulant:
I tell and finger it like Braille,
Gleaning the unsaid off the palpable,

And if I spy into its golden loops
I see us walk between the railway slopes
Into an evening of long grass and midges,
Blue smoke straight up, old beds and ploughs in hedges,
An auction notice on an outhouse wall –
You with a harvest bow in your lapel,

Me with the fishing rod, already homesick
For the big lift of these evenings, as your stick
Whacking the tips off weeds and bushes
Beats out of time, and beats, but flushes
Nothing: that original townland
Still tongue-tied in the straw tied by your hand.

The end of art is peace
Could be the motto of this frail device
That I have pinned up on our deal dresser –
Like a drawn snare
Slipped lately by the spirit of the corn
Yet burnished by its passage, and still warm.

SLOE GIN

The clear weather of juniper
darkened into winter.
She fed gin to sloes
and sealed the glass container.

When I unscrewed it
I smelled the disturbed

tart stillness of a bush
rising through the pantry.

When I poured it
it had a cutting edge
and flamed
like Betelgeuse.

I drink to you
in smoke-mirled, blue-black,
polished sloes, bitter
and dependable.

from CLEARANCES

3

When all the others were away at Mass
I was all hers as we peeled potatoes.
They broke the silence, let fall one by one
Like solder weeping off the soldering iron:
Cold comforts set between us, things to share
Gleaming in a bucket of clean water.
And again let fall. Little pleasant splashes
From each other's work would bring us to our senses.

So while the parish priest at her bedside
Went hammer and tongs at the prayers for the dying
And some were responding and some crying
I remembered her head bent towards my head,
Her breath in mine, our fluent dipping knives –
Never closer the whole rest of our lives.

4

Fear of affectation made her affect
Inadequacy whenever it came to
Pronouncing words 'beyond her'. *Bertold Brek.*
She'd manage something hampered and askew
Every time, as if she might betray
The hampered and inadequate by too
Well-adjusted a vocabulary.
With more challenge than pride, she'd tell me, 'You
Know all them things.' So I governed my tongue
In front of her, a genuinely well-
adjusted adequate betrayal
Of what I knew better. I'd *naw* and *aye*
And decently relapse into the wrong
Grammar which kept us allied and at bay.

7

In the last minutes he said more to her
Almost than in all their life together.
'You'll be in New Row on Monday night
And I'll come up for you and you'll be glad
When I walk in the door . . . Isn't that right?'
His head was bent down to her propped-up head.
She could not hear but we were overjoyed.
He called her good and girl. Then she was dead,
The searching for a pulsebeat was abandoned
And we all knew one thing by being there.
The space we stood around had been emptied
Into us to keep, it penetrated
Clearances that suddenly stood open.
High cries were felled and a pure change happened.

8

I thought of walking round and round a space
Utterly empty, utterly a source
Where the decked chestnut tree had lost its place
In our front hedge above the wallflowers.
The white chips jumped and jumped and skited high.
I heard the hatchet's differentiated
Accurate cut, the crack, the sigh
And collapse of what luxuriated
Through the shocked tips and wreckage of it all.
Deep planted and long gone, my coeval
Chestnut from a jam jar in a hole,
Its heft and hush become a bright nowhere,
A soul ramifying and forever
Silent, beyond silence listened for.

THE HAW LANTERN

The wintry haw is burning out of season,
crab of the thorn, a small light for small people,
wanting no more from them but that they keep
the wick of self-respect from dying out,
not having to blind them with illumination.

But sometimes when your breath plumes in the frost
it takes the roaming shape of Diogenes
with his lantern, seeking one just man;
so you end up scrutinised from behind the haw
he holds up at eyelevel on its twig,
and you flinch before its bonded pith and stone,
its blood-prick that you wish would test and clear you,
its pecked-at ripeness that scans you, then moves on.

MICHAEL LONGLEY

b. 1939

NO CONTINUING CITY

My hands here, gentle, where her breasts begin,
My picture in her eyes –
It is time for me to recognise
This new dimension, my last girl.
So, to set my house in order, I imagine
Photographs, advertisements – the old lies,
The lumber of my soul –

All that is due for spring cleaning,
Everything that soul-destroys.
Into the open I bring
Girls who linger still in phototstat
(For whom I was so many different boys) –
I explode their myths before it is too late,
Their promises I detonate –

There is quite a lot that I can do . . .
I leave them – are they six or seven, two or three? –
Locked in their small geographies.
The hillocks of their bodies' lovely shires
(Whose all weathers I have walked through)
Acre by acre recede entire
To summer country.

From collision to eclipse their case is closed.
Who took me by surprise
Like comets first – now, failing to ignite,
They constellate such uneventful skies,
Their stars arranged each night

In the old stories
Which I successfully have diagnosed.

Though they momentarily survive
In my delays,
They neither cancel nor improve
My continuing city with old ways,
Familiar avenues to love –
Down my one-way streets (it is time to finish)
Their eager syllables diminish.

Though they call out from the suburbs
Of experience – they know how that disturbs! –
Or, already tending towards home,
Prepare to hitch-hike on the kerbs,
Their bags full of dear untruths –
I am their medium
And I take the words out of their mouths.

From today new hoardings crowd my eyes,
Pasted over my ancient histories
Which (I must be cruel to be kind)
Only gale or cloudburst now discover,
Ripping the billboard of my mind –
Oh, there my lovers,
There my dead no longer advertise.

I transmit from the heart a closing broadcast
To my girl, my bride, my wife-to-be –
I tell her she is welcome,
Advising her to make this last,
To be sure of finding room in me
(I embody bed and breakfast) –
To eat and drink me out of house and home.

SWANS MATING

Even now I wish that you had been there
Sitting beside me on the riverbank:
The cob and his pen sailing in rhythm
Until their small heads met and the final
Heraldic moment dissolved in ripples.
This was a marriage and a baptism,
A holding of breath, nearly a drowning,
Wings spread wide for balance where he trod,
Her feathers full of water and her neck
Under the water like a bar of light.

CARAVAN

A rickety chimney suggests
The diminutive stove,
Children perhaps, the pots
And pans adding up to love –

So much concentrated under
The low roof, the windows
Shuttered against snow and wind,
That you would be magnified

(If you were there) by the dark,
Wearing it like an apron
And revolving in your hands
As weather in a glass dome,

The blizzard, the day beyond
And – tiny, barely in focus –
Me disappearing out of view
On probably the only horse,

Cantering off to the right
To collect the week's groceries,
Or to be gone for good
Having drawn across my eyes

Like a curtain all that light
And the snow, my history
Stiffening with the tea towels
Hung outside the door to dry.

IN MEMORIAM

My father, let no similes eclipse
Where crosses like some forest simplified
Sink roots into my mind, the slow sands
Of your history delay till through your eyes
I read you like a book. Before you died,
Re-enlisting with all the broken soldiers
You bent beneath your rucksack, near collapse,
In anecdote rehearsed and summarised
These words I write in memory. Let yours
And other heartbreaks play into my hands.

Now I see in close-up, in my mind's eye,
The cracked and splintered dead for pity's sake
Each dismal evening predecease the sun,
You, looking death and nightmare in the face
With you kilt, harmonica and gun,
Grow older in a flash, but none the wiser
(Who, following the wrong queue at The Palace,
Have joined the London Scottish by mistake),
Your nineteen years uncertain if and why
Belgium put the kibosh on the Kaiser.

Between the corpses and the soup canteens
You swooned away, watching your future spill.
But, as it was, your proper funeral urn
Had mercifully smashed to smithereens,
To shrapnel shards that sliced your testicle.
That instant I, your most unlikely son,
In No Man's Land was surely left for dead,
Blotted out from your far horizon.
As your voice now is locked inside my head,
I yet was held secure, waiting my turn.

Finally, that lousy war was over.
Stranded in France and in need of proof
You hunted down experimental lovers,
Persuading chorus girls and countesses:
This father, the last confidence you spoke.
In my twentieth year your old wounds woke
As cancer. Lodging under the same roof
Death was a visitor who hung about,
Strewing the house with pills and bandages
Till he chose to put your spirit out.

Though they overslept the sequence of events
Which ended with the ambulance outside,
You lingering in the hall, your bowels on fire,
Tears in your eyes, and all your medals spent,
I summon girls who packed at last and went
Underground with you. Their souls again on hire,
Now those lost wives as re-created brides
Take shape before me, materialise.
On the verge of light and happy legend
They lift their skirts like blinds across your eyes.

WOUNDS

Here are two pictures from my father's head –
I have kept them like secrets until now:
First, the Ulster Division at the Somme
Going over the top with 'Fuck the Pope!',
'No Surrender!': a boy about to die,
Screaming 'Give 'em one for the Shankill!'
'Wilder than Gurkhas' were my father's words
Of admiration and bewilderment.
Next comes the London-Scottish padre
Resettling kilts with his swagger-stick,
With a stylish backhand and a prayer.
Over a landscape of dead buttocks
My father followed him for fifty years.
At last, a belated casualty,
He said – lead traces flaring till they hurt –
'I am dying for King and Country, slowly.'
I touched his hand, his thin head I touched.

Now, with military honours of a kind,
With his badges, his medals like rainbows,
His spinning compass, I bury beside him
Three teenage soldiers, bellies full of
Bullets and Irish beer, their flies undone.
A packet of Woodbines I throw in,
A lucifer, the Sacred Heart of Jesus
Paralysed as heavy guns put out
The night-light in a nursery for ever;
Also a bus-conductor's uniform –
He collapsed beside his carpet-slippers
Without a murmur, shot through the head
By a shivering boy who wandered in
Before they could turn the television down

Or tidy away the supper dishes.
To the children, to a bewildered wife,
I think 'Sorry, Missus' was what he said.

FLEANCE

I entered with a torch before me
And cast my shadow on the backcloth
Momentarily: a handful of words,
One bullet with my initials on it –
And that got stuck in a property tree.

I would have caught it between my teeth
Or, a true professional, stood still
While the two poetic murderers
Pinned my silhouette to history
In a shower of accurate daggers.

But as any illusionist might
Unfasten the big sack of darkness,
The ropes and handcuffs, and emerge
Smoking a nonchalant cigarette,
I escaped – only to lose myself.

It took me a lifetime to explore
The dusty warren beneath the stage
With its trap door opening on to
All that had happened above my head
Like noises-off or distant weather.

In the empty auditorium I bowed
To one preoccupied caretaker
And, without removing my make-up,
Hurried back to the digs where Banquo
Sat up late with a hole in his head.

MAN LYING ON A WALL

homage to L.S. Lowry

You could draw a straight line from the heels,
Through calves, buttocks and shoulder blades
To the back of the head: pressure points
That bear the enormous weight of the sky.
Should you take away the supporting structure
The result would be a miracle or
An extremely clever conjuring trick.
As it is, the man lying on the wall
Is wearing the serious expression
Of popes and kings in their final slumber,
His deportment not dissimilar to
Their stiff, reluctant exits from this world
Above the shoulders of the multitude.

It is difficult to judge whether or not
He is sleeping or merely disinclined
To arrive punctually at the office
Or to return home in time for his tea.
He is wearing a pinstripe suit, black shoes
And a bowler hat: on the pavement
Below him, like a relic or something
He is trying to forget, his briefcase
With everybody's initials on it.

THE LINEN INDUSTRY

Pulling up flax after the blue flowers have fallen
And laying our handfuls in the peaty water
To rot those grasses to the bone, or building stooks
That recall the skirts of an invisible dancer,

148

We become a part of the linen industry
And follow its processes to the grubby town
Where fields are compacted into window boxes
And there is little room among the big machines.

But even in our attic under the skylight
We make love on a bleach green, the whole meadow
Draped with material turning white in the sun
As though snow reluctant to melt were our attire.

What's passion but a battering of stubborn stalks,
Then a gentle combing out of fibres like hair
And a weaving of these into christening robes,
Into garments for a marriage or funeral?

Since it's like a bereavement once the labour's done
To find ourselves last workers in a dying trade,
Let flax be our matchmaker, our undertaker,
The provider of sheets for whatever the bed –

And be shy of your breasts in the presence of death,
Say that you look more beautiful in linen
Wearing white petticoats, the bow on your bodice
A butterfly attending the embroidered flowers.

PEACE

after Tibullus

Who was responsible for the very first arms deal –
The man of iron who thought of marketing the sword?
Or did he intend us to use it against wild animals
Rather than ourselves? Even if he's not guilty

Murder got into the bloodstream as gene or virus
So that now we give birth to wars, short cuts to death.
Blame the affluent society: no killings when
The cup on the dinner table was made of beechwood,
And no barricades or ghettos when the shepherd
Snoozed among sheep that weren't even thoroughbreds.

I would like to have been alive in the good old days
Before the horrors of modern warfare and warcries
Stepping up my pulse rate. Alas, as things turn out
I've been press-ganged into service, and for all I know
Someone's polishing a spear with my number on it.
God of my Fathers, look after me like a child!
And don't be embarrassed by this handmade statue
Carved out of bog oak by my great-great-grandfather
Before the mass production of religious art
When a wooden god stood simply in a narrow shrine.

A man could worship there with bunches of early grapes,
A wreath of whiskery wheat-ears, and then say Thank you
With a wholemeal loaf delivered by him in person,
His daughter carrying the unbroken honeycomb.
If the good Lord keeps me out of the firing line
I'll pick a porker from the steamy sty and dress
In my Sunday best, a country cousin's sacrifice.
Someone else can slaughter enemy commanders
And, over a drink, rehearse with me his memoirs,
Mapping the camp in wine upon the table top.

It's crazy to beg black death to join the ranks
Who dogs our footsteps anyhow with silent feet –
No cornfields in Hell, nor cultivated vineyards,
Only yapping Cerberus and the unattractive
Oarsman of the Styx: there an anaemic crew
Sleepwalks with smoky hair and empty eye sockets.

How much nicer to have a family and let
Lazy old age catch up on you in your retirement,
You keeping track of the sheep, your son of the lambs,
While the woman of the house puts on the kettle.

I want to live until the white hairs shine above
A pensioner's memories of better days. Meanwhile
I would like peace to be my partner on the farm,
Peace personified: oxen under the curved yoke;
Compost for the vines, grape-juice turning into wine,
Vintage years handed down from father to son;
Hoe and ploughshare gleaming, while in some dark corner
Rust keeps the soldier's grisly weapons in their place;
The labourer steering his wife and children home
In a hay cart from the fields, a trifle sozzled.

Then, if there are skirmishes, guerrilla tactics,
It's only lovers quarrelling, the bedroom door
Wrenched off its hinges, a woman in hysterics,
Hair torn out, cheeks swollen with bruises and tears –
Until the bully-boy starts snivelling as well
In a pang of conscience for his battered wife:
Then sexual neurosis works them up again
And the row escalates into a war of words.
He's hard as nails, made of sticks and stones, the chap
Who beats his girlfriend up. A crime against nature.

Enough, surely, to rip from her skin the flimsiest
Of negligees, ruffle that elaborate hairdo,
Enough to be the involuntary cause of tears –
Though upsetting a sensitive girl when you sulk
Is a peculiar satisfaction. But punch-ups,
Physical violence, are out: you might as well
Pack your kitbag, goose-step a thousand miles away

From the female sex. As for me, I want a woman
To come and fondle my ears of wheat and let apples
Overflow between her breasts. I shall call her Peace.

THE THIRD LIGHT

The sexton is opening up the grave,
Lining with mossy cushions and couch grass
This shaft of light, entrance to the earth
Where I kneel to marry you again,
My elbows in darkness as I explore
From my draughty attic your last bedroom.
Then I vanish into the roof space.

I have handed over to him your pain
And your preference for Cyprus sherry,
Your spry quotations from the *Daily Mail*
With its crossword solved in ink, your limp
And pills, your scatter of cigarette butts
And last-minute humorous spring-cleaning
Of a corner of a shelf in his cupboard.

You spent his medals like a currency,
Always refusing the third light, afraid
Of the snipers who would extinguish it.
Waiting to scramble hand in hand with him
Out of the shell hole, did you imagine
A Woodbine passing to and fro, a face
That stabilises like a smoke ring?

AN AMISH RUG

As if a one-room schoolhouse were all we knew
And our clothes were black, our underclothes black,
Marriage a horse and buggy going to church
And the children silhouettes in a snowy field,

I bring you this patchwork like a smallholding
Where I served as the hired boy behind the harrow,
Its threads the colour of cantaloupe and cherry
Securing hay bales, corn cobs, tobacco leaves.

You may hang it on the wall, a cathedral window,
Or lay it out on the floor beside our bed
So that whenever we undress for sleep or love
We shall step over it as over a flowerbed.

GHETTO

I

Because you will suffer soon and die, your choices
Are neither right nor wrong: a spoon will feed you,
A flannel keep you clean, a toothbrush bring you back
To your bathroom's view of chimneypots and gardens.
With so little time for inventory or leave-taking,
You are packing now for the rest of your life
Photographs, medicines, a change of underwear, a book,
A candlestick, a loaf, sardines, needle and thread.
These are your heirlooms, perishables, worldly goods.
What you bring is the same as what you leave behind,
Your last belonging a list of your belongings.

II

As though it were against the law to sleep on pillows
They have filled a cathedral with confiscated feathers:
Silence irrefrangible, no room for angels' wings,
Tons of feathers suffocating cherubim and seraphim.

III

The little girl without a mother behaves like a mother
With her rag doll to whom she explains fear and anguish,
The meagreness of the bread ration, how to make it last,
How to get back to the doll's house and lift up the roof
And, before the flame-throwers and dynamiters destroy it,
How to rescue from their separate rooms love and sorrow,
Masterpieces the size of a postage stamp, small fortunes.

IV

From among the hundreds of thousands I can imagine one
Behind the barbed-wire fences as my train crosses Poland.
I see him for long enough to catch the sprinkle of snowflakes
On his hair and school bag, and then I am transported
Away from that world of broken hobbyhorses and silent toys.
He turns into a little snowman and refuses to melt.

V

For street-singers in the marketplace, weavers, warp-makers,
Those who suffer in sewing-machine repair shops, excrement-
Removal workers, there are not enough root vegetables,
Beetroots, turnips, swedes, nor for the leather-stitchers
Who are boiling leather so that their children may eat;
Who are turning like a thick slice of potato bread
This page, which is everything I know about potatoes,
My delivery of Irish Peace, Beauty of Hebron, Home
Guard, Arran Banners, Kerr's Pinks, resistant to eelworm,
Resignation, common scab, terror, frost, potato-blight.

VI

There will be performances in the waiting room, and time
To jump over a skipping rope, and time to adjust
As though for a dancing class the ribbons in your hair.
This string quartet is the most natural thing in the world.

VII

Fingers leave shadows on a violin, harmonics,
A blackbird that flutters between electrified fences.

VIII

Lessons were forbidden in that terrible school.
Punishable by death were reading and writing
And arithmetic, so that even the junior infants
Grew old and wise in lofts studying these subjects.
There were drawing lessons, and drawings of kitchens
And farms, farm animals, butterflies, mothers, fathers
Who survived in crayon until in pen and ink
They turned into guards at executions and funerals,
Torturing and hanging even these stick figures.
There were drawings of barracks and latrines as well
And the only windows were the windows they drew.

SEAMUS DEANE

b. 1940

RETURN

The train shot through the dark.
Hedges leapt across the windowpane.
Trees belled in foliage were stranded,
Inarticulate with rain.
A blur of lighted farm implied
The evacuated countryside.

I am appalled by its emptiness.
Every valley glows with pain
As we run like a current through;
Then the memories darken again.
In this Irish past I dwell
Like sound implicit in a bell.

The train curves round a river,
And how tenderly its gouts of steam
Contemplate the nodding moon
The waters from the clouds redeem.
Two hours from Belfast
I am snared in my past.

Crusts of light lie pulsing
Diamanté with the rain
At the track's end. Amazing!
I am in Derry once again.
Once more I turn to greet
Ground that flees from my feet.

ROOTS

Younger,
I felt the dead
Drag at my feet
Like roots
And at every step
I heard them
Crying
Stop.

Older,
I heard the roots
Snap. The crying
Stopped. Ever since
I have been
Dying
Slowly
From the top.

A SCHOOLING

Ice in the school room, listen,
The high authority of the cold
On some November morning
Turning to fragile crystals
In the Government milk
I was drinking and my world
All frost and snow, chalk and ice;
Quadratic equations on the board
Shining and shifting in white
Isosceles steps. In that trance
What could I know of his labour?

157

I, in my infinitesimally perceptive dance,
Thought nothing of the harbour
Where, in his fifth hour,
Waist-deep in water,
He laid cables, rode the dour
Iron swell between his legs
And maybe thought what kind of son,
An aesthetician of this cold,
He had, in other warmth, begot?
But there's ice in the school room,
Father. Listen. The harbour's empty.
The Government's milk has been drunk.
It lies on the stomach yet, freezing,
Its kindness, inhuman, has sunk
In where up starts the feeling
That pitches a cold in the thought
Of authority's broken milk crystals
On the lips of the son you begot.

FORDING THE RIVER

Sunday afternoon and the water
Black among the stones, the forest
Ash-grey in its permanent dusk
Of unquivering pine. That day
You unexpectedly crossed the river.

It was cold and you quickly shouted
As your feet felt the wet white stones
Knocking together. I had bent
To examine a strand of barbed wire
Looping up from a buried fence

When I heard you shout. And,
There you were, on the other side,
Running away. In a slow puncturing
Of anticipation I shivered
As if you had, unpermitted, gone for ever,

Gone, although you were already in the middle
Coming back; I picked up
Your shoes with a sense that years
Had suddenly decided to pass.
I remembered your riddle

On the way up here. ' "Brother or sister
I have none, but that man's father
Is my father's son." Who am I
Talking about?' About my son,
Who crossed cold Lethe, thought it Rubicon.

THE BRETHREN

Arraigned by silence, I recall
The noise of lecture rooms,
School refectories and dining hall,
A hundred faces in a hundred spoons,
Raised in laughter or in prayer bent,
Each distorted and each innocent.

Torrential sunlight falling through the slats
Made marquetries of light upon the floor.
I still recall those greasy Belfast flats
Where parties hit upon a steady roar
Of subdued violence and lent
Fury to the Sabbath which we spent

Hung over empty streets where Jimmy Witherspoon
Sang under the needle old laments
Of careless love and the indifferent moon,
Evoked the cloudy drumbrush scents
Of Negro brothels while our Plymouth Brethren,
Two doors down, sat sunk in heaven.

Stupor Sunday, *stupor mundi*. What was to come?
The plaints that were growing
Their teeth in the jaws of their aquarium
Sunday's splashless, deep-sown
Peace? What if it were shattered?
Our noise was life and life mattered.

Recently I found old photographs
Fallen behind the attic water tank
And saw my friends were now the staffs
Of great bureaucracies. Some frames stank
Of mildew, some were so defaced
That half the time I couldn't put a face

On half of them. Some were dead.
The water had seeped through a broken housing,
Had slowly savaged all those eyes and heads.
I felt its rusted coldness dousing
Those black American blues-fired tunes,
The faces echoed in those hammered spoons.

A BURIAL

The broken sods, a whipped flag,
The broad river beyond. Gunfire;
The young graves blotted all over.

Angels of morning light dance
On the silver needles of the estuary.
The helicopter prowls, a dragonfly
Popping its shuttered eyes.

Here we have a pause before rain,
And the clatter of clay
Feet on the porch of heaven.

In the stripped rain we wonder
What is going on here.
The cloudburst seems elegy enough.
Drooked shadows raise

White cellophaned flowers
In the darkened air.
Others kneel one-kneed

On a handkerchief. Cars
Glisten. Cameras at full exposure
Click. *Zeiss* and *Leica*
Whirr like crickets. Someone folds

A pistol in waterproof.
He is about to start his dry life,
This one, under the earth roof,

Tunnelling to his companions
In the honeycomb below
That weakens, with its intricacy,
The earth we hide in now.

HISTORY LESSONS

for Ronan Sheehan and Richard Kearney

'The proud and beautiful city of Moscow
Is no more.' So wrote Napoleon to the Czar.
It was a November morning when we came
On this. I remember the football pitches
Beyond, stretched into wrinkles by the frost.
Someone was running across them, late for school,
His clothes scattered open by the wind.

Outside Moscow we had seen
A Napoleonic, then a Hitlerian dream
Aborted. The firegold city was burning
In the Kremlin domes, a sabred Wehrmacht
Lay opened to the bone, churches were ashen
Until heretics restored their colour
And their stone. Still that boy was running.

Fragrance of Christ, as in the whitethorn
Brightening through Lent, the stricken aroma
Of the Czars in ambered silence near Pavlovsk,
The smoking gold of icons at Zagorsk,
And this coal-smoke in the sunlight
Stealing over frost, houses huddled up in
Droves, deep drifts of lost

People. This was history, although the State
Exam confined Ireland to Grattan and allowed
Us roam from London to Moscow. I brought
Black gladioli bulbs from Samarkand
To flourish like omens in our cooler air;
Coals ripening in a light white as vodka.
Elections, hunger strikes and shots

Greeted our return. Houses broke open
In the season's heat and the bulbs
Burned in the ground. Men on ladders
Climbed into roselight, a roof was a swarm of fireflies
At dusk. The city is no more. The lesson's learned,
I will remember it always as a burning
In the heart of winter and a boy running.

DEREK MAHON

b. 1941

IN CARROWDORE CHURCHYARD

at the grave of Louis MacNeice

Your ashes will not stir, even on this high ground,
However the wind tugs, the headstones shake –
This plot is consecrated, for your sake,
To what lies in the future tense. You lie
Past tension now, and spring is coming round
Igniting flowers on the peninsula.

Your ashes will not fly, however the rough winds burst
Through the wild brambles and the reticent trees.
All we may ask of you we have. The rest
Is not for publication, will not be heard.
Maguire, I believe, suggested a blackbird
And over your grave a phrase from Euripides.

Which suits you down to the ground, like this churchyard
With its play of shadow, its humane perspective.
Locked in the winter's fist, these hills are hard
As nails, yet soft and feminine in their turn
When fingers open and the hedges burn.
This, you implied, is how we ought to live –

The ironical, loving crush of roses against snow,
Each fragile, solving ambiguity. So
From the pneumonia of the ditch, from the ague
Of the blind poet and the bombed-out town you bring
The all clear to the empty holes of spring,
Rinsing the choked mud, keeping the colours new.

AN UNBORN CHILD

I have already come to the verge of
Departure. A month or so and
I shall be vacating this familiar room.
Its fabric fits me almost like a glove
While leaving latitude for a free hand.
I begin to put on the manners of the world,
Sensing the splitting light above
My head, where in the silence I lie curled.

Certain mysteries are relayed to me
Through the dark network of my mother's body
While she sits sewing the white shrouds
Of my apotheosis. I know the twisted
Kitten that lies there sunning itself
Under the bare bulb, the clouds
Of goldfish mooning around upon the shelf –
In me these data are already vested.

I feel them in my bones – bones which embrace
Nothing, for I am completely egocentric.
The pandemonium of encumbrances
Which will absorb me, mind and senses –
Intricacies of the box and the rat race –
I imagine only. Though they linger and,
Like fingers, stretch until the knuckles crack,
They cannot dwarf the dimensions of my hand.

I must compose myself in the nerve centre
Of this metropolis, and not fidget –
Although sometimes at night, when the city
Has gone to sleep, I keep in touch with it,
Listening to the warm red water
Racing in the sewers of my mother's body –

Or the moths, soft as eyelids, or the rain
Wiping its wet wings on the windowpane.

And sometimes too, in the small hours of the morning
When the dead filament has ceased to ring –
After the goldfish are dissolved in darkness
And the kitten has gathered itself up into a ball
Between the groceries and the sewing,
I slip the trappings of my harness
To range these hollows in discreet rehearsal
And, battering at the concavity of my caul,

Produce in my mouth the words I WANT TO LIVE –
This my first protest, and shall be my last.
As I am innocent, everything I do
Or say is couched in the affirmative.
I want to see, hear, touch and taste
These things with which I am to be encumbered.
Perhaps I need not worry – give
Or take a day or two, my days are numbered.

THE SPRING VACATION

for Michael Longley

Walking among my own this windy morning
In a tide of sunlight between shower and shower,
I resume my old conspiracy with the wet
Stone and the unwieldy images of the squinting heart.
Once more, as before, I remember not to forget.

There is a perverse pride in being on the side
Of the fallen angels and refusing to get up.
We could *all* be saved by keeping an eye on the hill

166

At the top of every street, for there it is,
Eternally, if irrelevantly, visible –

But yield instead to the humorous formulae,
The hidden menace in the knowing nod.
Or we keep sullen silence in light and shade,
Rehearsing our astute salvations under
The cold gaze of sanctimonious God.

One part of my mind must learn to know its place.
The things that happen in the kitchen houses
And echoing backstreets of this desperate city
Should engage more than my casual interest,
Exact more interest than my casual pity.

ECCLESIASTES

God, you could grow to love it, God-fearing, God-
    chosen purist little puritan that,
for all your wiles and smiles, you are (the
    dank churches, the empty streets,
the shipyard silence, the tied-up swings) and
    shelter your cold heart from the heat
of the world, from woman-inquisition, from the
    bright eyes of children. Yes you could
wear black, drink water, nourish a fierce zeal
    with locusts and wild honey, and not
feel called upon to understand and forgive
    but only to speak with a bleak
afflatus, and love the January rains when they
    darken the dark doors and sink hard
into the Antrim hills, the bog-meadows, the heaped
    graves of your fathers. Bury that red

167

bandana and stick, that banjo, this is your
    country, close one eye and be king.
Your people await you, their heavy washing
    flaps for you in the housing estates –
a credulous people. God, you could do it, God
    help you, stand on a corner stiff
with rhetoric, promising nothing under the sun.

THE SNOW PARTY

for Louis Asekoff

Bashō, coming
To the city of Nagoya,
Is asked to a snow party.

There is a tinkling of china
And tea into china,
There are introductions.

Then everyone
Crowds to the window
To watch the falling snow.

Snow is falling on Nagoya
And farther south
On the tiles of Kyōto.

Eastward, beyond Irago,
It is falling
Like leaves on the cold sea.

Elsewhere they are burning
Witches and heretics
In the boiling squares,

Thousands have died since dawn
In the service
Of barbarous kings –

But there is silence
In the houses of Nagoya
And the hills of Ise.

THE LAST OF THE FIRE KINGS

I want to be
Like the man who descends
At two milk churns

With a bulging
String bag and vanishes
Where the lane turns,

Or the man
Who drops at night
From a moving train

And strikes out over the fields
Where fireflies glow
Not knowing a word of the language.

Either way, I am
Through with history –
Who lives by the sword

Dies by the sword.
Last of the fire kings, I shall
Break with tradition and

Die by my own hand
Rather that perpetuate
The barbarous cycle.

Five years I have reigned
During which time
I have lain awake each night

And prowled by day
In the sacred grove
For fear of the usurper,

Perfecting my cold dream
Of a place out of time,
A palace of porcelain

Where the frugivorous
Inheritors recline
In their rich fabrics
Far from the sea.

But the fire-loving
People, rightly perhaps,
Will not countenance this,

Demanding that I inhabit,
Like them, a world of
Sirens, bin lids
And bricked-up windows –

Not to release them
From the ancient curse
But to die their creature and be thankful.

POEM BEGINNING WITH A LINE BY CAVAFY

It is night
And the barbarians have not come.
It was not always so hard;
When the great court flared
With gallowglasses and language difficulty
A man could be a wheelwright and die happy.

We remember
Oatmeal and mutton,
Harpsong, a fern table for
Wiping your hands on,
A candle of reeds and butter,
The distaste of the rheumatic chronicler,

A barbarous tongue
And herds like cloud-shadow
Roaming the wet hills
When the hills were young,
Whiskery pikemen and their spiky dogs
Preserved in woodcuts and card catalogues.

Now it is night
And the barbarians have not come,
Or if they have we only recognise,
Harsh as a bombed bathroom,
The frantic anthropologisms
And lazarous ironies

Behind their talk
Of fitted carpets, central
Heating and automatic gear change –
Like the bleached bones of a hare
Or a handful of spent
Cartridges on a deserted rifle range.

BRUCE ISMAY'S SOLILOQUY

They said I got away in a boat
And humbled me at the inquiry. I tell you
    I sank as far that night as any
Hero. As I sat shivering on the dark water
    I turned to ice to hear my costly
Life go thundering down in a pandemonium of
    Prams, pianos, sideboards, winches,
Boilers bursting and shredded ragtime. Now I hide
    In a lonely house behind the sea
Where the tide leaves broken toys and hatboxes
    Silently at my door. The showers of
April, flowers of May mean nothing to me, nor the
    Late light of June, when my gardener
Describes to strangers how the old man stays in bed
    On seaward mornings after nights of
Wind, and will see no one, repeat no one. Then it is
    I drown again with all those dim
Lost faces I never understood. My poor soul
    Screams out in the starlight, heart
Breaks loose and rolls down like a stone.
    Include me in your lamentations.

A REFUSAL TO MOURN

He lived in a small farmhouse
At the edge of a new estate.
The trim gardens crept
To his door, and car engines
Woke him before dawn
On dark winter mornings.

All day there was silence
In the bright house. The clock
Ticked on the kitchen shelf,
Cinders moved in the grate,
And a warm briar gurgled
When the old man talked to himself;

But the doorbell seldom rang
After the milkman went,
And if a coat hanger
Knocked in an open wardrobe
That was a strange event
To be pondered on for hours

While the wind thrashed about
In the back garden, raking
The roof of the henhouse,
And swept clouds and gulls
Eastwards over the lough
With its flap of tiny sails.

Once a week he would visit
An old shipyard crony,
Inching down to the road
And the blue country bus
To sit and watch sun-dappled
Branches whacking the windows

While the long evening shed
Weak light in his empty house,
On the photographs of his dead
Wife and their six children
And the Missions to Seamen angel
In flight above the bed.

'I'm not long for this world,'
Said he on our last evening,
'I'll not last the winter',
And grinned, straining to hear
Whatever reply I made;
And died the following year.

In time the astringent rain
Of those parts will clean
The words from his gravestone
In the crowded cemetery
That overlooks the sea
And his name be mud once again

And his boilers lie like tombs
In the mud of the sea bed
Till the next ice age comes
And the earth he inherited
Is gone like Neanderthal Man
And no records remain.

But the secret bred in the bone
On the dawn strand survives
In other times and lives,
Persisting for the unborn
Like a claw-print in concrete
After the bird has flown.

A DISUSED SHED IN CO. WEXFORD

Let them not forget us, the weak souls among the asphodels.
                                        Seferis, *Mythistorema*

for J. G. Farrell

Even now there are places where a thought might grow –
Peruvian mines, worked out and abandoned
To a slow clock of condensation,
An echo trapped for ever, and a flutter of
Wildflowers in the lift shaft,
Indian compounds where the wind dances
And a door bangs with diminished confidence,
Lime crevices behind rippling rainbarrels,
Dog corners for bone burials;
And in a disused shed in Co. Wexford,

Deep in the grounds of a burnt-out hotel,
Among the bathtubs and the washbasins
A thousand mushrooms crowd to a keyhole.
This is the one star in their firmament
Or frames a star within a star.
What should they do there but desire?
So many days beyond the rhododendrons
With the world waltzing in its bowl of cloud,
They have learnt patience and silence
Listening to the rooks querulous in the high wood.

They have been waiting for us in a foetor of
Vegetable sweat since civil war days,
Since the gravel-crunching, interminable departure
Of the expropriated mycologist.
He never came back, and light since then
Is a keyhole rusting gently after rain.
Spiders have spun, flies dusted to mildew,

And once a day, perhaps, they have heard something –
A trickle of masonry, a shout from the blue
Or a lorry changing gear at the end of the lane.

There have been deaths, the pale flesh flaking
Into the earth that nourished it;
And nightmares, born of these and the grim
Dominion of stale air and rank moisture.
Those nearest the door grow strong –
Elbow room! Elbow room!
The rest, dim in a twilight of crumbling
Utensils and broken pitchers, groaning
For their deliverance, have been so long
Expectant that there is left only the posture.

A half century, without visitors, in the dark –
Poor preparation for the cracking lock
And creak of hinges. Magi, moonmen,
Powdery prisoners of the old regime,
Web-throated, stalked like triffids, racked by drouth
And insomnia, only the ghost of a scream
At the flashbulb firing squad we wake them with
Shows there is life yet in their feverish forms.
Grown beyond nature now, soft food for worms,
They lift frail heads in gravity and good faith.

They are begging us, you see, in their wordless way,
To do something, to speak on their behalf
Or at least not to close the door again.
Lost people of Treblinka and Pompeii!
Save us, save us, they seem to say,
Let the god not abandon us
Who have come so far in darkness and in pain.
We too had our lives to live.
You with your light meter and relaxed itinerary,
Let not our naïve labours have been in vain!

COURTYARDS IN DELFT

PIETER DE HOOCH, 1659

for Gordon Woods

Oblique light on the trite, on brick and tile –
Immaculate masonry, and everywhere that
Water tap, that broom and wooden pail
To keep it so. House-proud, the wives
Of artisans pursue their thrifty lives
Among scrubbed yards, modest but adequate.
Foliage is sparse, and clings. No breeze
Ruffles the trim composure of those trees.

No spinet-playing emblematic of
The harmonies and disharmonies of love;
No lewd fish, no fruit, no wide-eyed bird
About to fly its cage while a virgin
Listens to her seducer, mars the chaste
Precision of the thing and the thing made.
Nothing is random, nothing goes to waste:
We miss the dirty dog, the fiery gin.

That girl with her back to us who waits
For her man to come home for his tea
Will wait till the paint disintegrates
And ruined dykes admit the esurient sea;
Yet this is life too, and the cracked
Outhouse door a verifiable fact
As vividly mnemonic as the sunlit
Railings that front the houses opposite.

I lived there as a boy and know the coal
Glittering in its shed, late-afternoon
Lambency informing the deal table,
The ceiling cradled in a radiant spoon.

177

I must be lying low in a room there,
A strange child with a taste for verse,
While my hard-nosed companions dream of war
On parched veldt and fields of rain-swept gorse;

For the pale light of that provincial town
Will spread itself, like ink or oil,
Over the not yet accurate linen
Map of the world which occupies one wall
And punish nature in the name of God.
If only, now, the Maenads, as of right,
Came smashing crockery, with fire and sword,
We could sleep easier in our beds at night.

ACHILL

im chaonaí uaigneach nach mór go bhfeicim an lá

I lie and imagine a first light gleam in the bay
    After one more night of erosion and nearer the grave,
Then stand and gaze from a window at break of day
    As a shearwater skims the ridge of an incoming wave;
And I think of my son a dolphin in the Aegean,
    A sprite among sails knife-bright in a seasonal wind,
And wish he were here where currachs walk on the ocean
    To ease with his talk the solitude locked in my mind.

I sit on a stone after lunch and consider the glow
    Of the sun through mist, a pearl bulb containèdly fierce;
A rain-shower darkens the schist for a minute or so
    Then it drifts away and the sloe-black patches disperse.
Croagh Patrick towers like Naxos over the water
    And I think of my daughter at work on her difficult art
And wish she were with me now between thrush and plover,
    Wild thyme and sea-thrift, to lift the weight from my heart.

The young sit smoking and laughing on the bridge at evening
  Like birds on a telephone pole or notes on a score.
A tin whistle squeals in the parlour, once more it is raining,
  Turfsmoke inclines and a wind whines under the door;
And I lie and imagine the lights going on in the harbour
  Of white-housed Náousa, your clear definition at night,
And wish you were here to upstage my disconsolate labour
  As I glance through a few thin pages and switch off the light.

TOM MATTHEWS

b. 1945

PRIVATE BUT SULPHUROUS

My time he said was not my own
I had so much to do I was up at dawn

What with relations and friends
    and friends of relations
In the end they simply exhausted my patience

No more, I said to them all one day
No more for now, I am going on holiday
I wasn't of course, I was going away to stay

And I built this villa on Vesuvius
It is private here but sulphurous

HAPPY ARABIA

'I speak for the world of scholarship'
    he said
'For knowledge for knowledge's sake'

And when the poet clutched his ankle
And murmured in delirium of Eden
He delivered him a lecture on its etymology

The poet heard only the words
Arabia Eudaimon

Arabia Felix
Happy Arabia

Oh happy happy happy Arabia

ROBERT SAT

The congregation was scandalised
When Robert sat in his pew and read a paperback

My mother said afterwards
'If he wasn't interested why did he come'

And I marvelled at her
For she never thought of applying that criterion
    to me

And I marvelled at Robert too
Able to read so calmly in the midst of so much
    hate

Robert is now doing very nicely thank you
He emigrated to Canada
And broke both legs in a skiing accident
And married a nurse

COWBOY FILM

When asked her opinion
The old lady said

The horses were wrong
You never saw a white horse

And the children's teeth were wrong
Children had rotten teeth in those days

And the women were very wrong

Another thing she said was the smell
But you cannot expect films to smell

EVEN THE WHALES

Even the whales now
communicate sparingly with staccato cries
Polyphony was yesterday's song
We are minimalists
now, even the whales.

MICHAEL FOLEY

b. 1947

from TRUE LIFE LOVE STORIES

16

Sois sage, ô ma doleur . . . I don't
   hate the young any more.
Let them greet with satirical
   signs of the cross

and smirk of their 'impecunious state'.
   I won't hate them
any more. Love's the boyo to
   see them all straight,

so I muse, for I'm soft as an
   inside leg this year
all due to woman's passive power.
   Entends, ma chère,

this song and soft clip-clop is me.
   It's you I trot to,
tired and tame, melodious with
   new-found gallantry.

19

The sword is a cold bride. Yuk!
   I need the warmth
of fragrant human flesh (though I
   wouldn't deny our

good times on the march – untainted
   self-reliant band).
Ah comrades, it is time to say goodbye.
   If you could see

her you would understand. *She is*
   beautiful then? Yes
she is beautiful. Sad sighs and
   nods. We file outside,

still hushed observe the ancient soothing
   stars. *She will await*
you. Go to her. Firm Roman hand-
   shakes all round.

29

Ah no, ah no, they weren't all gross and slow.
   The message didn't
just read GO. There were many amusing
   men in that land –

they'd mostly failed but there it's
   what a man must do.
It's not the place for enterprise
   (their have-a-go grocer

got his head blown off). I'll miss its
   forty shades of spleen,
slouching off with my own, un-
   repentant churl.

It's *an honour* to merit
   the 'misfit' tag –
A felon's cap's the finest crown
   an Irish head can wear.

184

LUCKY EUGENE

a teaching poem

And the graduates can't stand the college-trained staff.
And the college-trained staff have their own way to scoff:

They expect a piece of paper to see them through.
But they both despise the lab. tech. – though it's due

To 'professional standing' and not a mere whim.
Choicer professions can't stand them. They can't stand him.

Eugene's the lab. technician. He's a non-staff grade
And that means no staff room for Eugene, I'm afraid!

NO markers of homework sharing funny mistakes.
NO epic anecdoters fouling coffee breaks.

NO dangerous after-schoolers wild with work-itch
(Lay their poor bones to rest in the all-weather pitch).

NO daddy-mad teasers, so hateful and thrilling
('Risk it for a biscuit', 'Willing for a shilling').

And NO teachers' jargon – (the boss not a 'slob'
But 'a one-ulcer man in a two-ulcer job').

Lucky Eugene locked in the lab. beyond dislike
Blasting through *The Decline and Fall of the Third Reich!*

It's a bad scene, Euge, unromantic on the blurb
And as far as you can get from DO NOT DISTURB.

A PROVINCIAL ADOLESCENCE

His nights in the aunts' house, their talk and tea:
who can trace a line back like they can?
They cover the district faster than Tarzan
family tree to family tree

and keep track of their own who're away
– Father Tim's tapes from the Far East:
It's O'Doherty's mince I miss most.
Laughter. Shrieks. It's as good as a play.

They prefer it like this, indoors, the fire on
with their three-tiered cake stands for three-course snacks
legs apart, enjoying the crack
(he fancies the youngest one).

'Don't be getting an eye for the girls whatever you do.
Get all your degrees
and they'll be running after *you*.'
They give him a briefcase for getting an A and two Bs.

Are there men by any chance?
The men doze in chairs
while the women sort out their affairs
– an extreme case of aunts-in-the-pants.

And in summer the big two-car day trips
aunts crammed in the back, at the wheel glum men.
The men have no say in destination or stops.
They have to bolt their ice cream and drive on again.

BROTHERS AND SISTERS

No, not writers for Heaven's sake. That bunch of slobbers
    Are nobody's brothers.
    It's a secret, I shouldn't say
    But they're mostly *t..h..i..c..k.*
They've read little, know less. Sick, sour and full of booze
    They're locked out of Heaven
    And nothing consoles them, not even
    The big print their prestigious publishers use.

My brothers rarely write though they've intelligence and fun.
    Most jobs have one
    Tucked away, detached and wry
    Knowing just when to catch your eye
During a.o.b. at the AGM as they move to split the motion
    Into five separate parts
    Before debating and voting starts
    A motion on methods of coffee-money collection.

Or at those lovely moments when people give the game away
    Some status-seeker, say
    Affecting to scorn petty worry
    For love of jokes, Indian curry
Parties, booze and sex – *until someone else gets promotion*
    When you glimpse the real man
    Beneath the Monty Python fan
    Such flashes of revelation the headiest potion.

How they love wisdom, my brothers, open to any question
    Yet full of discretion
    Never trying to make you booze
    Pressure and lack of time excused
(We'll be free in a better age, as Cavafy used to say).
    Like icebergs, with seven-eighths below

187

But not cold as icebergs. No, no
Warm, the warmth coming through in its indirect way.

And sisters? Those as well, discussing the usual bothers
      Husbands and lovers
      Who go or won't go, stay or won't stay
      Awkward and hurtful either way.
Women always tell you more, not obsessed with hiding pain.
      Instead of the usual bland crap
      Genuine goodies fall in your lap
    Bizarre, funny and intimate knowledge of men.

The warmth was direct then. It would make a sated prince moan
      The sweet nights I've known.
      They've jostled the post-sherry queue
      To get next to me at the staff do
Flesh fragrant with good scent, carefully made-up and dressed
      Not just agreeing with, *fancying* too
      Turning my insides to warm goo
    Eyes locked on mine, holding them, really impressed.

THE MIDDLE MANAGER IN PARADISE

Homeostasis finally. System oscillation over. All parameters at
    rest.
I have my eternal reward for doing my best

Well earned, with squeezes and cuts and harmonious working
    relations to foster
In a time of eroded differentials and deficit-staffing posture

With regular breakdown of normative order, colleagues who
    couldn't care less

A total absence of structured complementarity in the interaction
  process.

Here it is at last – peace and space with nothing to spoil it
Like running out of tins or having to empty a chemical toilet

And if solitude and empty places give me the blues
There's the first nights, launchings, openings and anniversary
  dos.

No need to panic, heaping your plate at the smorgasbord
You can go back as many times as you like and nobody says a
  word

Unlimited red/white, sweet/dry sploshing out of your glass in
  the fray
Crushed up against beautiful women who, far from turning
  away

Agree to oral sex when accosted, taking on all comers
And serving them any number of times (single swallows don't
  make summers).

Every taste is catered for. There's cut-price SM centres stocking
  every line
Braziers, branding irons, manacles, self-assembly torture racks
  in natural pine.

Though no one's exploited really and of course there's no
  brutality.
Everyone has meaningful relationships and is comfortable in
  their sexuality.

We have consciousness-raising sessions and state-of-the-art
  seminars

Regular small encounter groups to find and remove whatever
jars

Recurrent education preventing crises from catching us
napping
Creating autonomous learners geared to continuous
environment-shaping.

No one's exempt from our in-service training. Every six weeks
You attend a hands-on workshop in troubleshooting techniques

Simulated stress situations assessed by Barry, the young whizz
kid:
'I think you were a *shade too directive* there, Ken . . . *unless of course
it was a leadership bid.'*

Barry will keep us results-oriented. Barry won't let us get lax
And take refuge in cognitive dissonance (refusing to face facts)

And anyway God's always popping in to see if everything's
all right
Distinguished and reassuring, goateed, with the voice of an
acting knight

Showing interest, concern and civility (so much rarer and harder
than love)
And signing his humorous bestselling autobiography *Heavens
Above!*

ON THE WATERFRONT

There can be no such thing as a life
that wasn't meant for the person who has it.

Louis Simpson

We think our loved ones pull us under
    So unfairly
Interfering with demands that end our
    High hopes early.
I could have been a contender.
    It was you, Charlie.

We're always handed loaded dice
    In this vale of woe.
It's not your night, kid. We're going for the price.
    How well we know
Charlie's unignorable advice.
    – But is it so?

Could Terry have taken Wilson apart
    As he thought?
Did he really have the heart
    For a title shot
– Or were we biased from the start
    By a strong crude plot?

You should never blame an outcome
    On conditions
Or people. When you end up a bum
    Breeding pigeons
Accept the fault's your own dumb
    Cowardly decisions.

FRANK ORMSBY

b. 1947

WINTER OFFERINGS

Mother, it pains me that I must confide
To verse these clarities. We're each alone.
Our speech gutters. More than marriage divides
Us. Each visit home
I measure distances and find them grown.

It's your own fault, really. My good at heart
You grasped the chances that would sunder us.
I'm glad you chose to play the dogged part,
Take on the opposition. Often I wonder
How you prevailed against that blunderbuss

My father. What-was-good-enough-for-him –
The peasant's caution rather than a ploy
To keep me tethered; but you saw how grim
The prospects. Trapped yourself, you rescued me
From lives I guess at. Then, how could I joy

In love so functional, how call it love
That hid and whispered in a tough concern
With Grants and Benefits? So, schooled above
You, I grew up to miss those transferred yearnings.
School's out, but now in retrospect I learn.

Discarded woman, shame is turning me
To wish you mornings, and a folding night
Whose dreams are gentle, sight enough to see
This late guest bowed with winter offerings
Who turns his face into your going light.

A DAY IN AUGUST

And still no stronger. Swathed in rugs he lingered
   Near to the windows, gauging distant hills.
Balked by the panes that promised light and flowers,
   The wasps were dying furiously on sills.

A doctor called. She walked him to the doorstep,
   Then sent the children out to gather cones
Under the trees beside the ruined churchyard.
   They romped, unheeding, in the tilted stones.

And now the wheels are turning. They impress
   Tracks that will not outlast the winter's rain.
The siren leaves a wash of emptiness.
   He is lost to the small farms, lane by lane.

SPOT THE BALL

Once, with a certain pride, we kept attempts
To the minimum. Reason was all:
To trace invisibly the upraised eyes
Of backs and forwards; where the lines converged
To plant our crosses.

Later we combed the stand advertisements
For smudged lettering, or held the thin page
Up to the light to test for shadow.
Those paler patches, blotches near the goal
Could well be erasions.

And, later still, the joking nonchalance,
The stray marks in all the wrong places,

Floodlights and flags and corners that the teams
Had turned their backs on. Even the goalie's crutch
Was not immune.

Four years now and never on the right end
Of a Snowball. Thursday's edition tells
Of prizes bound for places elsewhere.
The 'Belfast man who requests no publicity'
Is always another.

We persevere from habit. When we try
These days our hope's mechanical, we trust
To accident. We are selective
No longer, the full hundred crosses
Filling the sky.

THE WAR PHOTOGRAPHERS

Working with one eye closed or heads buried
under their drapes, they focus to preserve
the drowned shell hole, the salient's rubble of dead,
the bleached bones of sepoys torn from the earth.

Their stills haunt us: a stretcher piled with skulls
at Cold Harbour, graves in a barren wood
that in one hour's carnage lost its name
to history and the world's memory of death.

The worst has happened, they confirm the worst:
but show us too the makeshift hospital,
the sad errand of the hospital van
among the ruins. Also enough of sky
to suggest the infinity of angles,

that behind sandbags, under the hostile towers
someone is finding time for a wry note
on bowel movements, an entry that affirms
the loved salience of what is always there:
flower of Auschwitz, bird of the Western Front.

from A NORTHERN SPRING

13 APPLES, NORMANDY, 1944

Was it D + 10 or D + 12 we caught
the war artist sketching apples?

'I'm sick of tanks,' he said. 'I'm sick of ruins.
I'm sick of dead soldiers and soldiers on the move
and soldiers resting.
And to tell you the truth, I'm sick drawing refugees.
I want to draw apples.'

For all we know he's still sitting under a tree
somewhere between the Seine and Omaha,
or, russet with pleasure, striding past old dugouts
towards the next windfall –
sketchbooks accumulating as he becomes
the Audubon of French apples,

or works on the single apple
– perfect, planetary – of his imagination.

30 SOLDIER BATHING

The bigger fish have country cousins here.
At their own depth sonaghen and gillaroo
dart in the quiet loughs and are not found elsewhere.

I dry on the shore and imagine the world renewed
cleanly between two islands I cannot name:
as a rounded stone, say, that the ebb left bare,
or light on water the morning after a war.

HOME

Once, in the Giant's Ring, I closed my eyes
and thought of Ireland,
the air-wide, skintight, multiple meaning of here.

When I opened them I was little the wiser,
in that, perhaps, one
with the first settlers in the Lagan Valley
and the Vietnamese boat-people of Portadown.

CIARAN CARSON

b. 1948

BELFAST CONFETTI

Suddenly as the riot squad moved in, it was raining
   exclamation marks,
Nuts, bolts, nails, car keys. A fount of broken type. And the
   explosion
Itself – an asterisk on the map. This hyphenated line, a burst of
   rapid fire . . .
I was trying to complete a sentence in my head, but it kept
   stuttering,
All the alleyways and side streets blocked with stops and
   colons.

I know this labyrinth so well – Balaclava, Raglan, Inkerman,
   Odessa Street –
Why can't I escape? Every move is punctuated. Crimea Street.
   Dead end again.
A Saracen, Kremlin-2 mesh. Makrolon face-shields. Walkie-
   talkies. What is
My name? Where am I coming from? Where am I going? A
   fusillade of question marks.

CAMPAIGN

They had questioned him for hours. Who exactly was he?
   And when
He told them, they questioned him again. When they accepted
   who he was, as
Someone not involved, they pulled out his fingernails. Then

They took him to a waste ground somewhere near the
    Horseshoe Bend, and told him
What he was. They shot him nine times.

A dark umbilicus of smoke was rising from a heap of burning
    tyres.
The bad smell he smelt was the smell of himself. Broken glass
    and knotted Durex.
The knuckles of a face in a nylon stocking. I used to see him in
    the Gladstone Bar,
Drawing pints for strangers, his almost-perfect fingers flecked
    with scum.

THE MOUTH

There was this head had this mouth he kept shooting off.
    Unfortunately.
It could have been worse for us than it was for him.
    Provisionally.
But since nothing in this world is certain and you don't know
    who hears what
We thought it was time he bit off more than he could chew.
    Literally.
By the time he is found there'll be nothing much left to tell
    who he was.

But of course some clever dick from the 'Forscenic Lab'
    reconstructs
Him, what he used to be – not from his actual teeth, not his
    fingerprints,
But from the core – the toothmarks of the first and last bite
    he'd taken of
This sour apple. But then we would have told them anyway.
    Publicity.

THE KNEE

His first bullet is a present, a mark of intelligence that will
End in the gutter behind The Clock Bar, since he keeps on
   doing what
He's not supposed to. The next one is for real, what we've just
   talked about.
It seems he was a hood, whatever, or the lads were just being
   careful.
Two and two were put together; what they added up to
   wasn't five.

Visiting time: he takes his thirteen-month-old son on his
   other knee.
Learning to walk, he suddenly throws himself into the
   staggering
Distance between his father and his father's father, hands
   held up high,
His legs like the hands of a clock, one trying to catch up on
   the other.

DRESDEN

Horse Boyle was called Horse Boyle because of his brother
   Mule;
Though why Mule was called Mule is anybody's guess. I
   stayed there once,
Or rather, I nearly stayed there once. But that's another story.
At any rate they lived in this decrepit caravan, not two miles
   out of Carrick,
Encroached upon by baroque pyramids of empty baked bean
   tins, rusts
And ochres, hints of autumn merging into twilight. Horse
   believed

They were as good as a watchdog, and to tell you the truth
You couldn't go near the place without something falling
    over:
A minor avalanche would ensue – more like a shop bell,
    really,

The old-fashioned ones on string, connected to the latch, I
    think,
And as you entered in, the bell would tinkle in the empty
    shop, a musk
Of soap and turf and sweets would hit you from the gloom.
    Tobacco.
Baling wire. Twine. And, of course, shelves and pyramids of
    tins.
An old woman would appear from the back – there was a
    sizzling pan in there,
Somewhere, a whiff of eggs and bacon – and ask you what
    you wanted;
Or rather, she wouldn't ask; she would talk about the weather.
    It had rained
That day, but it was looking better. They had just put in the
    spuds.
I had only come to pass the time of day, so I bought a token
    packet of Gold Leaf.
All this time the fry was frying away. Maybe she'd a daughter
    in there
Somewhere, though I hadn't heard the neighbours talk of it; if
    anybody knew,
It would be Horse. Horse kept his ears to the ground.
And he was a great man for current affairs; he owned the only
    TV in the place.
Come dusk he'd set off on his rounds, to tell the whole
    townland the latest
Situation in the Middle East, a mortar bomb attack in
    Mullaghbawn –

The damn things never worked, of course – and so he'd tell
the story
How in his young day it was very different. Take young
Flynn, for instance,
Who was ordered to take this bus and smuggle some sticks of
gelignite

Across the border, into Derry, when the RUC – or was it the
RIC? –
Got wind of it. The bus was stopped, the peeler stepped on.
Young Flynn
Took it like a man, of course: he owned up right away. He
opened the bag
And produced the bomb, his rank and serial number. For all
the world
Like a pound of sausages. Of course, the thing was, the
peeler's bike
Had got a puncture, and he didn't know young Flynn from
Adam. All he wanted
Was to get home for his tea. Flynn was in for seven years and
learned to speak
The best of Irish. He had thirteen words for a cow in heat;
A word for the third thwart in a boat, the wake of a boat on
the ebb tide.

He knew the extinct names of insects, flowers, why this place
was called
Whatever: *Carrick*, for example, was *a rock*. He was damn
right there –
As the man said, *When you buy meat you buy bones, when you
buy land you buy stones.*
You'd be hard put to find a square foot in the whole bloody
parish
That wasn't thick with flints and pebbles. To this day he could
hear the grate

And scrape as the spade struck home, for it reminded him of
  broken bones:
Digging a graveyard, maybe – or better still, trying to dig a
  reclaimed tip
Of broken delph and crockery ware – you know that sound
  that sets your teeth on edge
When the chalk squeaks on the blackboard, or you shovel
  ashes from the stove?

Master McGinty – he'd be on about McGinty then, and
  discipline, the capitals
Of South America, Moore's *Melodies*, the Battle of Clontarf,
  and
Tell me this, an educated man like you: What goes on four legs when
  it's young,
Two legs when it's grown up, and three legs when it's old? I'd
  pretend
I didn't know. McGinty's leather strap would come up then,
  stuffed
With threepenny bits to give it weight and sting. Of course, it
  never did him
Any harm: *You could take a horse to water but you couldn't make*
  him drink.
He himself was nearly going on to be a priest.
And many's the young cub left the school, as wise as when he came.

Carrowkeel was where McGinty came from – *Narrow Quarter*,
  Flynn explained –
Back before the Troubles, a place that was so mean and
  crabbed,
Horse would have it, men were known to eat their dinner
  from a drawer.
Which they'd slide shut the minute you'd walk in.
He'd demonstrate this at the kitchen table, hunched and
  furtive, squinting

Out the window – past the teetering minarets of rust, down
    the hedge-dark aisle –
To where a stranger might appear, a passer-by, or what was
    maybe worse
Someone he knew. Someone who wanted something.
    Someone who was hungry.
Of course who should come tottering up the lane that instant
    but his brother
Mule. I forgot to mention they were twins. They were as like
    two –
No, not peas in a pod, for this is not the time nor the place to
    go into
Comparisons, and this is really Horse's story, Horse who –
    now I'm getting
Round to it – flew over Dresden in the war. He'd emigrated
    first, to
Manchester. Something to do with scrap – redundant mill
    machinery,
Giant flywheels, broken looms that would, eventually, be
    ships, or aeroplanes.
He said he wore his fingers to the bone.
And so, on impulse, he had joined the RAF. He became a rear
    gunner.
Of all the missions, Dresden broke his heart. It reminded him
    of china.

As he remembered it, long afterwards, he could hear, or
    almost hear
Between the rapid desultory thunderclaps, a thousand
    tinkling echoes –
All across the map of Dresden, storerooms full of china
    shivered, teetered
And collapsed, an avalanche of porcelain, slushing and
    cascading: cherubs,

Shepherdesses, figurines of Hope and Peace and Victory,
     delicate bone fragments.
He recalled in particular a figure from his childhood, a
     milkmaid
Standing on the mantelpiece. Each night as they knelt down
     for the rosary,
His eyes would wander up to where she seemed to beckon to
     him, smiling,
Offering him, eternally, her pitcher of milk, her mouth of rose
     and cream.

One day, reaching up to hold her yet again, his fingers
     stumbled, and she fell.
He lifted down a biscuit tin, and opened it.
It breathed an antique incense: things like pencils, snuff,
     tobacco.
His war medals. A broken rosary. And there, the milkmaid's
     creamy hand, the outstretched
Pitcher of milk, all that survived. Outside, there was a
     scraping
And a tittering; I knew Mule's step by now, his careful
     drunken weaving
Through the tin-stacks. I might have stayed the night, but
     there's no time
To go back to that now; I could hardly, at any rate, pick up the
     thread.
I wandered out through the steeples of rust, the gate that was
     a broken bed.

THE IRISH FOR NO

Was it a vision, or a waking dream? I heard her voice before I
     saw

204

What looked like the balcony scene in *Romeo and Juliet*,
     except Romeo
Seemed to have shinned up a pipe and was inside arguing
     with her. The casements
Were wide open and I could see some Japanese-style wall-
     hangings, the dangling
Quotation marks of a yin-yang mobile. *It's got nothing*, she
     was snarling, *nothing*
To do with politics, and, before the bamboo curtain came
     down,
That goes for you too!

It was time to turn into the dog's-leg short cut from Chlorine
     Gardens
Into Cloreen Park, where you might see an *Ulster Says No*
     scrawled on the side
Of the power-block – which immediately reminds me of the
     Eglantine Inn
Just on the corner: on the missing *h* of Cloreen, you might
     say. We were debating,
Bacchus and the pards and me, how to render *The Ulster Bank –
     the Bank*
That Likes to Say Yes into Irish, and whether eglantine was
     alien to Ireland.
I cannot see what flowers are at my feet, when *yes* is the verb
     repeated,
Not exactly yes, but phatic nods and whispers. *The Bank That
     Answers All*
Your Questions, maybe? That Greek portico of Mourne granite,
     dazzling
With promises and feldspar, mirrors you in the Delphic black
     of its windows.

And the bruised pansies of the funeral parlour are dying in
     reversed gold letters,

The long sigh of the afternoon is not yet complete on the
    promontory where the victim,
A corporal in the UDR from Lisbellaw, was last seen having
    driven over half
Of Ulster, a legally held gun was found and the incidence of
    stress came up
On the headland which shadows Larne Harbour and the
    black pitch of warehouses.
There is a melancholy blast of diesel, a puff of smoke which
    might be black or white.
So the harbour slips away to perilous seas as things remain
    unsolved; we listen
To the *ex cathedra* of the foghorn, and *drink and leave the world
    unseen* –

What's all this to the Belfast businessman who drilled
Thirteen holes in his head with a Black & Decker? It was just
    a normal morning
When they came. The tennis court shone with dew or frost, a
    little before dawn.
The border, it seemed, was not yet crossed: the Milky Way
    trailed snowy brambles,
The stars clustered thick as blackberries. They opened the door
    into the dark:
The murmurous haunt of flies on summer eves. Empty jam jars.
Mish-mash. Hotch-potch. And now you rub your eyes and get
    acquainted with the light
A dust of something reminiscent drowses over the garage
    smell of creosote,
The concrete: blue clouds in porcelain, a paint brush steeped
    in a chipped cup;
Staples hyphenate a wet cardboard box as the upturned can of
    oil still spills
And the unfed cat toys with the yin-yang of a tennis ball,
    debating whether *yes* is *no*.

206

The first indication was this repeated tic, the latch jigging and
    clicking
As he rehearsed the possibility of entering, or opening. Maybe
It was a knock, a question; Uncle John was not all there. Yet
    he had
His father's eyes, his mother's nose; and I myself, according to
    my mother,
Had his mouth. I would imagine speaking for him sometimes.
    He had
A second cousin's hands, or a cousin's twice removed, an
    uncle's way of walking:
In other words, he was himself. So he might walk in this very
    minute, or turn
His back on us to contemplate the yellow brick edgings of the
    bricked-in
Windows of the mill wall opposite. He seemed to see things
    that we didn't
See: cloud-shadow eddying and swirling round a manhole;
    the bits of grit
That glittered at the edges; individual as dirt, the dog-leg walk
    of a dog
As it followed its nose from one side of the street to the other.
    His ears
Might prick to the clatter of an empty tin kicked down an
    entry,
Diminishing the yelps of children as their skipping rope
    became a blur,
Then slowed and stopped, then whipped back up again, the
    up-hill down-dale
Quickening pulse of a cardiograph. We watched him hover
    and dilate
In the frosted glass. Someone would get up; he would retreat.
    An electric

Yellow bakery van hummed by; he sniffed the air. A car
   backfired.
Like the fast-forward or the rewind button, everything is
   going far too
Fast, though we might know precisely, having heard it all
   before for real,
What is going on, like that climactic moment of a rounded,
   oratorical
Gesture, practised in the mirror till it seemed completely
   unfamiliar:
The hyped-up, ninety-to-the-dozen commentary that
   illustrates, in retrospect,
The split-second when a goal is scored; the laid-back, bit-by-
   bit analysis
As we take in every slowed-down motion of the replay. We
   are looking
For a piece we know is there, amongst the clutter and the
   glug of bottles,
Whispering, the chink of loose change, the unfamiliar voices
   that are us
And cloud our hearing. The repeated melancholic parp of a
   car horn
Eventually has heralded the moment: now we know what's
   coming next, the voice
Hoarsened by the second-generation tape, the echo of a
   nearly empty, dusty
Concert hall, illuminated, we imagine, by the voice, one shaft
   of fitful sunlight
That retreated almost instantly to a nimbo-cumulus – gold-
   edged, slate-blue,
Glimmering between its cup and lip – imponderably
   weighing on the skylight.
A yellow bakery van hums by. There is a lull, and then a car
   backfires.

It's getting nearer now, that out-of-focus look he had: a
   wall-eye
With its yellowed white, the confused rainbow of the iris
   weeping unpredictably.
The tortoiseshell frame had one missing lens. Why they were
   bifocals
I don't know; he didn't read. Spinning yarns was more his
   line, always something
Off the top of his head. Or he might sing a song: perhaps *I'm
   going down the town*
*And I know who's going with me. I have a wee boy of my own, and
   his name is –*
Here he'd mention my name, which was almost my name;
   half of it, at least,
Was right. All this while he champed, between gulps of tea,
   two thick buttered
Doorsteps of a *Peter Pan* loaf, and cast his eye on the
   yellowed pages
Of an *Old Moore's Almanac* for 1948, the year, in fact, that I
   was born.
Storms this month, I see; hurricanes and thunder . . . the
   almanac was upside down,
But sure enough, just then, above the smoke-stack of the mill
   on up the street,
I caught a dark umbilicus of cloud, a momentary flash. Rain
   pattered on the window.
A yellow bakery van went by; he sniffed the ozone. A car
   backfired.

You can tell that this was all some time ago, although it does
   repeat itself.
On this particular day, my other uncle, Pat, had just come in
   from work.
He plunked two loaves down on the table. A doughy-sour
   inveterate smell

Breathed out from him, and as he lifted off the white cloud of
     his cap, it sparked off
The authoritative onset of this other, needle-in-the-haystack
     day that I
Began with. That ratchety delay with which the clock is
     poised, conjugating
All its tensed-up coils and springs: rain pattered on the
     window. An electric
Yellow bakery van whirred off. A car backfired. Someone
     seemed to get up very
Slowly. A dog was barking. The car backfired again. Every-
     thing was getting faster
And the door bursts open. He is babbling, stammering,
     contractions
Getting nearer, nearer, all the blips run into one another till
     they are
A wave, a wall: *They said to push, she pushed, they said to shut her
     mouth,*
*She pushed, they said to keep her head down, and she pushed once
     more –*
The wave has almost broken – *more, they said*: a lock of hair, a
     bald patch,
Hair again. Flecks of blood and foam. He cannot get it all out
     fast enough.

Afterwards, a lull. He sits up and he takes a cup of tea, a slice
     of toast.
He is himself again, though I can see myself in him. *I remember
     very well*, he says,
When you were born; oh yes, thunder, hurricanes; and as I see the
     bruised
Posthumous violet of his face, I hear him talk about the shape
     of this particular
Cloud he saw last week, or this dog he'd noticed last week,
     which he'd imitate,

210

Panting, slabbering and heaving as it lolled about the margins
of the new estate –
Nettles, yellow chickweed, piss-the-beds – sniffing, wagging,
following itself
Back through that remembered day of complex perfume, a
trail of moments
Dislocated, then located. This dog. That bitch. There is a long-
forgotten
Whimper, a groan of joy as it discovers home: a creosoted
hutch, a bowl,
The acrid spoor of something that was human.

HAMLET

As usual, the clock in The Clock Bar was a good few minutes
fast:
A fiction no one really bothered to maintain, unlike the story
The comrade on my left was telling, which no one knew for
certain truth:
*Back in 1922, a sergeant, I forget his name, was shot outside the
National Bank . . .*
Ah yes, what year was it that they knocked it down? Yet, its
memory's as fresh
As the inky smell of new pound notes – which interferes with
the beer-and-whiskey
Tang of now, like two dogs meeting in the revolutionary '69 of
a long sniff,
Or cattle jostling shit-stained flanks in the Pound. For *pound,*
as some wag
Interrupted, was an offshoot of the Falls, from the Irish, *fál,* a
hedge;
Hence, *any kind of enclosed thing,* its twigs and branches
commemorated

By the soldiers' drab and olive camouflage, as they try to melt
Into a brick wall; red coats might be better, after all. *At any
    rate,*
*This sergeant's number came up; not a winning one. The bullet had
    his name on it.*
Though Sergeant x, as we'll call him, doesn't really feature in
    the story:
The nub of it is. *This tin can which was heard that night,
    trundling down*
*From the bank, down Balaclava Street. Which thousands
    heard, and no one ever*
Saw. Which was heard for years, any night that trouble might be
Round the corner . . . and when it skittered to a halt, you knew
That someone else had snuffed it: a name drifting like an
    afterthought,
A scribbled wisp of smoke you try and grasp, as it becomes
    diminuendo, then
Vanishes. For *fál* is also *frontier, boundary*, as in the *undiscovered
    country*
From whose bourne no traveller returns, the illegible, thorny
    hedge of time itself –
Heartstopping moments, measured not by the pulse of a
    wristwatch, nor
The archaic anarchists' alarm clock, but a mercury tilt device
Which 'only connects' on any given bump on the road. So, by
    this wingèd messenger
The promise 'to pay the bearer' is fulfilled:

As someone buys another round, an Allied Irish Bank ten-
    pound note drowns in
The slops of the counter; a Guinness stain blooms on the
    artist's impression
Of the sinking of the *Girona*; a tiny foam hisses round the
    salamander brooch

Dredged up to show how love and money endure, beyond
    death and the Armada,
Like the bomb-disposal expert in his suit of salamander-cloth.
Shielded against the blast of time by a strangely medieval
    visor,
He's been outmoded by this jerky robot whose various
    attachments include
A large hook for turning over corpses that may be booby-trapped;
But I still have this picture of his hands held up to avert the
    future
In a final act of *No surrender,* as, twisting through the murky
    fathoms
Of what might have been, he is washed ashore as pearl and
    coral.

This *strange eruption to our state* is seen in other versions of
    the Falls:
A no-go area, a ghetto, a demolition zone. For the ghost, as it turns
    out –
All this according to your man, and I can well believe it – this
    tin ghost,
Since the streets it haunted were abolished, was never heard
    again.
The sleeve of Raglan Street has been unravelled; the helmet of
    Balaclava
Is torn away from the mouth. The dim glow of Garnet has
    gone out,
And with it, all but the memory of where I lived. I, too, heard
    the ghost:
A roulette trickle, or the hesitant annunciation of a downpour,
    ricocheting
Off the window; a goods train shunting distantly into a siding,
Then groaning to a halt; the rainy cries of children after dusk.
For the voice from the grave reverberates in others' mouths, as
    the sails

213

Of the whitethorn hedge swell up in a little breeze, and
  tremble
Like the spiral blossom of Andromeda: so suddenly are
  shrouds and branches
Hung with streetlights, celebrating all that's lost, as fields are
  reclaimed
By the Starry Plough. So we name the constellations, to put a
  shape
On what was there; so, the storyteller picks his way between
  the isolated stars.
But, *Was it really like that?* And, *Is the story true?*
You might as well tear off the iron mask, and find that no one,
  after all,
Is there: nothing but a cry, a summons, clanking out from the
  smoke
Of demolition. Like some son looking for his father, or the
  father for his son,
We try to piece together the exploded fragments. Let these
  broken spars
Stand for the Armada and its proud full sails, for even if
The clock is put to rights, everyone will still believe it's fast:
The barman's shouts of *time* will be ignored in any case, since
  time
Is conversation; it is the hedge that flits incessantly into the
  present,
As words blossom from the speakers' mouths, and the flotilla
  returns to harbour,
Long after hours.

TOM PAULIN

b. 1949

SETTLERS

They cross from Glasgow to a black city
  Of gantries, mills and steeples. They begin to belong.
He manages the Iceworks, is an elder of the Kirk;
  She becomes, briefly, a cook in Carson's Army.
Some mornings, walking through the company gate,
  He touches the bonnet of a brown lorry.
It is warm. The men watch and say nothing.
  'Queer, how it runs off in the night,'
He says to McCullough, then climbs to his office.
  He stores a warm knowledge on his palm.

Nightlandings on the Antrim coast, the movement of guns
  Now snug in their oiled paper below the floors
Of sundry kirks and tabernacles in that county.

UNDER THE EYES

Its retributions work like clockwork
Along murdering miles of terrace houses
Where someone is saying, 'I am angry,
I am frightened, I am justified.
Every favour, I must repay with interest,
Any slight against myself, the least slip,
Must be balanced out by an exact revenge.'

The city is built on mud and wrath.
Its weather is predicted; its streetlamps

Light up in the glowering, crowded evenings.
Time-switches, ripped from them, are clamped
To sticks of sweet, sweating explosive.
All the machinery of a state
Is a set of scales that squeezes out blood.

Memory is just, too. A complete system
Nothing can surprise. The dead are recalled
From school room afternoons, the hill quarries
Echoing blasts over the secured city;
Or, in a private house, a Judge
Shot in his hallway before his daughter
By a boy who shut his eyes as his hand tightened.

A rain of turds; a pair of eyes; the sky and tears.

PERSONAL COLUMN

These messages are secret, the initials
Code them, puzzling most of us. 'LY
Where are you now? I love you still. MN.'
And then, next evening, 'MN are you still there?
Loving you. LY.' Until, 'Shall I write
To old address?' MN suggests, waiting.

Each teatime, the thin signals start again.
You can almost hear the cheeping
Of separated loves, obscure adulteries
That finished in pub car parks, though they want
To make it new, to meet again, furtively,
Like spies whose thoughts touch before their bodies can.

Love, in an empty warehouse, might be like this.
To think small print, so public, can be tender.
Who'd guess that in a city where the news
Is normal, so many men and women wait
For the paperboy, their go-between, to bring them
Lonely but hopeful, to a bed somewhere?

A LYRIC AFTERWARDS

There was a taut dryness all that summer
and you sat each day in the hot garden
until those uniformed comedians
filled the street with their big white ambulance,
fetching you and bringing you back to me.

Far from the sea of ourselves we waited
and prayed for the tight blue silence to give.
In your absence I climbed to a square room
where there were dried flowers, folders of sonnets
and crossword puzzles: call them musical

snuffboxes or mannered anachronisms,
they were all too uselessly intricate,
caskets of the dead spirit. Their bitter
constraints and formal pleasures were a style
of being perfect in despair; they spoke

with the vicious trapped crying of a wren.
But that is changed now, and when I see you
walking by the river, a step from me,
there is this great kindness everywhere:
now in the grace of the world and always.

CADAVER POLITIC

The grey hills of that country fall away
    Like folds of skin. There are some mountains somewhere
And public parks with metal fountains.
    Rains fall and then fogs freeze, drifting
Over empty stretches of water, forts
    With broken walls on small islands.
Rafted cities smoke in the rain and sharp posts
    Have been knocked deep into flabby ground,
Thin tatters of chicken wire strung to them.
    Coffins are moored in its bays and harbours.
A damp rag, it flies several flags –
    Bunting and boneyard streamers, the badges
Of territory. In the waste, silent valleys
    Clans are at their manoeuvres.
At the bottom of a cliff, on a tussock
    Of ground by a lean-to shed, a group
Of men and women huddle, watching a man
    Who tries, with damp matches, to light a board
Washed on that coast by the grey sea.

DESERTMARTIN

At noon, in the dead centre of a faith,
Between Draperstown and Magherafelt,
This bitter village shows the flag
In a baked absolute September light.
Here the Word has withered to a few
Parched certainties, and the charred stubble
Tightens like a black belt, a crop of Bibles.

Because this is the territory of the Law
I drive across it with a powerless knowledge –

The owl of Minerva in a hired car.
A Jock squaddy glances down the street
And grins, happy and expendable,
Like a brass cartridge. He is a useful thing,
Almost at home, and yet not quite, not quite.

It's a limed nest, this place. I see a plain
Presbyterian grace sour, then harden,
As a free strenuous spirit changes
To a servile defiance that whines and shrieks
For the bondage of the letter: it shouts
For the Big Man to lead his wee people
To a clean white prison, their scorched tomorrow.

Masculine Islam, the rule of the Just,
Egyptian sand dunes and geometry,
A theology of rifle-butts and executions:
These are the places where the spirit dies.
And now, in Desertmartin's sandy light,
I see a culture of twigs and bird-shit
Waving a gaudy flag it loves and curses.

THE OTHER VOICE

Anglican firelight.
Jugged hare in a stone house.
The gowned schoolmaster

Has a saintly politeness.
'It is possible to wonder,'
I hear him say.

219

The wind soughs in the demesne.
Exiles light a candle
To the gods of place.

In the winter darkness
Of this mild village
There is the mossy fragrance

Of damp branches under leaves,
The sour yeast of fungus.
At the lighted doorway

I forget to shake hands.
'We must meet again,' he calls,
And I pretend to pretend.

*

I make that crossing again
And catch the salt freshness
Of early light on Queen's Island.

I lay claim to those marshes,
The Lagan, the shipyards,
The Ormeau Road in winter.

That back room off Donegall Pass,
Remember, where the cell met?
That cupboard of books, tracts and poems?

Plekhanov flares like a firework,
Trotsky crosses Siberia
Turning the pages of Homer,

Raskolnikov wears a long coat
And the end justifies the means.
'Soon the rosewood *meubles*

'Will shake in the drawing rooms
On the Malone Road.
After the long marches

'There will be shares for us all
In the means of production.
Songs of a new society

'Will grow like flowers
From the barrel of a gun.
It's easy. It's easy.

'Love is all you need.'
The record sticks and the party
Spins on for ever.

                    *

We wished it could happen.
Less often now, I wish it still.
For it seems like a barren

Simplicity with no ghosts.
And those dreams of gardens
Called me from the way, saying:

'Here are the small mercies,
A glass of wine, the pungent shade,
And a cagy friendship.

'Grace is a volume of Horace,
Bishops and pigeons
Cooing in a woggles shire.

'Life, my dear, is a fixed order
And your verse should flow
With a touching sweetness.

'Better a civil twilight
Than the level emptiness
Of pulp culture.'

                    *

In the visions of the night
When deep sleep falls on men,
The flickering pictures

Pass before our eyes.
The fear of necessity
In an absolute narrative.

History is happening:
Tanks and caterpillars,
A moth lying in the dust.

'Once, in Odessa, I watched
The governor cursing.
His back was turned in the hot square.

'A regiment with bark sandals,
A sprig of green in their caps.
Their tragedy scorched my mind.

'Those bark sandals, those green sprigs!
But the process of history
Must scorn an emotion.

'I am history now.
I carry time in my mind.
As sharp as an axe.'

                    *

The actors shake their fists.
I hear the same opinions
In a muddy light.

I see a regiment of clones
Waving their arms and shouting:
A glossy brutalism dances

To a parody of song.
Identikit opinions
In the camps of the punks.

The theatre is in the streets,
The streets are in the theatre,
The poet is torn to pieces.

                    *

What does a poem serve?
Only the pure circle of itself.
Now, between two coasts,

The servants of the state
Doze to the drum of engines.
Hammered stars, a dark dream,

The hard night in a dead bowl.
Where a free light wakes
To its spacious language

Choice is still possible.
I dream of a subtle voice,
Stare in a mirror and pray

To a shadow wandering
Beyond the cold shores
And tides of the Baltic.

*

In Buddhist Moscow,
In lamp-eyed St Petersburg,
Mandelstam is walking

Through the terrible night.
His lips are moving
In the lyric ripple.

The syllables chirp
Like a dolphin, lost
In the grey depths of the state.

'As I walk through the dark
I will tell you this:
That morning, in the buttery

'Of the Kremlin, I left
Because I could never stay
In the same room as Trotsky.

'Do you understand me?
Those ideals will fit you
Like a feral uniform.

'Hear how the wolves howl,
Functions of nature
On the frozen plains.

'All the dry glitters
In your cento of memories
Will never catch

'The living truth on the wing.
The bird has flown its nest
And the snow weighs

'On the gothic branches,
Lavish and cruel, like power.
What cadences, what rich voices

'Have you hardened against?
What images have you broken?
In the great dome of art

'(It was this we longed for
In our Petropolis)
I am free of history.

'Beyond dust and rhetoric,
In the meadows of the spirit
I kiss the Word.'

MANICHEAN GEOGRAPHY I

Consider a coral or guano atoll
Where a breezy Union Jack
Flaps above the police station.

There is a rusting mission hut
Built out of flattened tin cans
(Bully beef, beans and tomato pilchards)

Where the Reverend Bungo Buller
And his prophet, Joe Gimlet,
Preach the gospel of cargoes.

They worship a white god
Of dentures and worn toothbrushes
Who will come to earth, Hallelulia,

In a reconditioned Flying Fortress
Humping bales of fresh calico
And a crate of Black and Deckers.

Seeding like brisk parachutes,
The ancestral spirits will fall
From the pod of an airship,

And the chosen people will serve
Themselves with orange jube-jubes
In a brand-new discount warehouse.

SURVEILLANCES

In the winter dusk
You see the prison camp

With its blank watchtowers;
It is as inevitable
As the movement of equipment
Or the car that carries you
Towards a violent district.

In the violet light
You watch a helicopter
Circling above the packed houses,
A long beam of light
Probing streets and waste ground.
All this might be happening
Underwater.

And if you would swap its functions
For a culture of bungalows
And light verse,
You know this is one
Of the places you belong in,
And that its public uniform
Has claimed your service.

AN ULSTER UNIONIST WALKS THE STREETS OF LONDON

All that Friday
there was no flag –
no Union Jack,
no tricolour–
on the governor's mansion.
I waited outside the gate lodge,
waited like a dog
in my own province
till a policeman brought me
a signed paper.

Was I meant to beg
and be grateful?
I sat on the breakfast-shuttle and I called –
I called out loud –
to the three Hebrew children
for I know at this time
there is neither prince, prophet, nor leader –
there is no power
we can call our own.
I grabbed a fast black –
ack, I caught a taxi –
to Kentish Town,
then walked the streets
like a half-foreigner
among the London Irish.
What does it feel like?
I wanted ask them –
what does it feel like
to be a child of that nation?
But I went underground
to the Strangers' House –

We vouch, they swore,
We deem, they cried,
till I said, 'Out . . .
I may go out that door
and walk the streets
searching my own people.'

MEDBH MCGUCKIAN

b. 1950

TULIPS

Touching the tulips was a shyness
I had had for a long time – such
Defensive mechanisms to frustrate the rain
That shakes into the sherry glass
Of the daffodil, though scarcely
Love's young dream; such present-mindedness
To double-lock in tiers as whistle-tight,
Or catch up on sleep with cantilevered
Palms cupping elbows. It's their independence
Tempts them to this grocery of soul.

Except, like all governesses, easily
Carried away, in sunny
Absences of mirrors they exalt themselves
To ballets of revenge, a kind
Of twinness, an olympic way of earning,
And are sacrificed to plot, their faces
Lifted many times to the artistry of light –
Its lovelessness a deeper sort
Of illness than the womanliness
Of tulips with their bee-dark hearts.

THE SOFA

Do not be angry if I tell you
Your letter stayed unopened on my table
For several days. If you were friend enough

229

To believe me, I was about to start writing
At any moment; my mind was savagely made up,
Like a serious sofa moved
Under a north window. My heart, alas,

Is not the calmest of places.
Still it is not my heart that needs replacing:
And my books seem real enough to me,
My disasters, my surrenders, all my loss . . .
Since I was child enough to forget
That you loathe poetry, you ask for some –
About nature, greenery, insects, and of course,

The sun – surely that would be to open
An already open window? Celebrating
The impudence of flowers? If I could
Interest you instead in his large, gentle stares,
How his soft shirt is the inside of pleasure
To me, why I must wear white for him,
Imagine he no longer trembles

When I approach, no longer buys me
Flowers for my name day . . . But I spread
On like a house, I begin to scatter
To a tiny to-and-fro at odds
With the wear on my threshold. Somewhere
A curtain rising wonders where I am,
My books sleep, pretending to forget me.

MR MCGREGOR'S GARDEN

Some women save their sanity with needles.
I complicate my life with studies

Of my favourite rabbit's head, his vulgar volatility,
Or a little ladylike sketching
Of my resident toad in his flannel box;
Or search for handsome fungi for my tropical
Herbarium, growing dry rot in the garden,
And wishing that the climate were kinder,
Turning over the spiky purple heads among the moss
With my cheese-knife to view the slimy veil.

Unlike the cupboard-love of sleepers in the siding,
My hedgehog's sleep is under his control
And not the weather's; he can rouse himself
At half an hour's notice in the frost, or leave at will
On a wet day in August, by the hearth.
He goes by breathing slowly, after a large meal,
A lively evening, very cross if interrupted,
And returns with a hundred respirations
To the minute, weak and nervous when he wakens,
Busy with his laundry.

On sleepless nights while learning
Shakespeare off by heart,
I feel that Bunny's at my bedside
In a white cotton nightcap,
Tickling me with his whiskers.

THE SEED-PICTURE

This is my portrait of Joanna – since the split
The children come to me like a dumbwaiter,
And I wonder where to put them, beautiful seeds
With no immediate application . . . the clairvoyance
Of seed-work has opened up
New spectrums of activity, beyond a second home.

The seeds dictate their own vocabulary,
Their dusty colours capture
More than we can plan,
The mould on walls, or jumbled garages,
Dead flower heads where insects shack . . .
I only guide them not by guesswork
In their necessary numbers,
And attach them by the spine to a perfect bedding,
Woody orange pips, and tear-drop apple,
The banana of the caraway, wrinkled peppercorns,
The pocked peach, or water lily honesty,
The seamed cherry stone so hard to break.

Was it such self-indulgence to enclose her
In the border of a grandmother's sampler,
Bonding all the seed in one continuous skin,
The sky resolved to a cloud the length of a man?
To use tan linseed for the trees, spiky
Sunflower for leaves, bright lentils
For the window, patna stars
For the floral blouse? Her hair
Is made of hook-shaped marigold, gold
Of pleasure for her lips, like raspberry grain.
The eyelids oatmeal, the irises
Of Dutch blue maw, black rape
For the pupils, millet
For the vicious beige circles underneath.
The single pearl barley
That sleeps around her dullness
Till it catches light, makes women
Feel their age, and sigh for liberation.

THE FLOWER MASTER

Like foxgloves in the school of the grass moon
We come to terms with shade, with the principle
Of enfolding space. Our scissors in brocade,
We learn the coolness of straight edges, how
To gently stroke the necks of daffodils
And make them throw their heads back to the sun.

We slip the thready stems of violets, delay
The loveliness of the hibiscus dawn with quiet ovals,
Spirals of feverfew like water splashing,
The papery legacies of bluebells. We do
Sea-fans with sea-lavender, moon-arrangements
Roughly for the festival of moon-viewing.

This black container calls for sloes, sweet
Sultan, dainty nipplewort, in honour
Of a special guest, who, summoned to the
Tea ceremony, must stoop to our low doorway,
Our fontanelle, the trout's dimpled feet.

THE FLITTING

'You wouldn't believe all this house has cost me –
In body-language terms, it has turned me upside down.'
I've been carried from one structure to the other
On a chair of human arms, and liked the feel
Of being weightless, that fraternity of clothes . . .
Now my own life hits me in the throat, the bumps
And cuts of the walls as telling
As the poreholes in strawberries, tomato seeds.
I cover them for safety with these Dutch girls

Making lace, or leaning their almond faces
On their fingers with a mandolin, a dreamy
Chapelled ease abreast this other turquoise-turbaned,
Glancing over her shoulder with parted mouth.

She seems a garden escape in her unconscious
Solidarity with darkness, clove-scented
As an orchid taking fifteen years to bloom,
And turning clockwise as the honeysuckle.
Who knows what importance
She attaches to the hours?
Her narrative secretes its own values, as mine might
If I painted the half of me that welcomes death
In a faggoted dress, in a peacock chair,
No falser biography than our casual talk
Of losing a virginity, or taking a life, and
No less poignant if dying
Should consist in more than waiting.

I postpone my immortality for my children,
Little rock-roses, cushioned
In long-flowering sea-thrift and metrics,
Lacking elemental memories:
I am well-earthed here as the digital clock,
Its numbers flicking into place like overgrown farthings
On a bank where once a train
Ploughed like an emperor living out a myth
Through the cambered flesh of clover and wild carrot.

ON NOT BEING YOUR LOVER

Your eyes were ever brown, the colour
Of time's submissiveness. Love nerves

234

Or a heart, beat in their world of
Privilege, I had not yet kissed you
On the mouth.

But I would not say, in my un-freedom
I had weakly drifted there, like the
Bone-deep blue that visits and decants
The eyes of our children:

How warm and well-spaced their dreams
You can tell from the sleep-late mornings
Taken out of my face! Each lighted
Window shows me cardiganed, more desolate
Than the garden, and more hallowed
Than the hinge of the brass-studded
Door that we close, and no one opens,
That we open and no one closes.

In a far-flung, too young part,
I remembered all your slender but
Persistent volume said, friendly, complex
As the needs of your new and childfree girl.

THE SITTING

My half-sister comes to me to be painted:
She is posing furtively, like a letter being
Pushed under a door, making a tunnel with her
Hands over her dull-rose dress. Yet her coppery
Head is as bright as a net of lemons, I am
Painting it hair by hair as if she had not
Disowned it, or forsaken those unsparkling
Eyes as blue may be sifted from the surface

Of a cloud; and she questions my brisk
Brushwork, the note of positive red
In the kissed mouth I have given her,
As a woman's touch makes curtains blossom
Permanently in a house: she calls it
Wishfulness, the failure of the tampering rain
To go right into the mountain, she prefers
My sea-studies, and will not sit for me
Again, something half-opened, rarer
Than railroads, a soiled red-letter day.

LITTLE HOUSE, BIG HOUSE

In a day or two the chairs will fall to pieces:
Those who were once lovers need the minimum
Of furniture, half-people, each with his separate sky.

Christmas peered through the escallonia hedge,
And passed almost unnoticed, except the stamps
Had squirrels on them. Why should I take
My apron off for a wineless dinner? My things
Are too grey, like a tree I deepen shadows
With my brown autumn raincoat.

On the ground floor, one room opens into another,
And a small Matisse in the inglenook
Without its wood fire is stroked by light
From north and south. That started all the feelings
That had slept till then, I came out
From behind the teapot to find myself
Cooled by a new arrangement of doorways
And choosing a spiced bun from a china shell.

A shawl no whiter than my white skin
Made me a dust jacket, I overwatered
The Michaelmas daisies thinking about
The clawlike bedroom door handles along
The minstrel's gallery. And the house like me
Was tangled with the emotion of cut flowers –

So different from an ordinary going-away –
That I could hardly keep my hand
From phoning you, impromptu. Since our blood
Is always older than we will ever be,
I should like to lie in Tarusa under matted winter grass,
Where the strawberries are redder than anywhere else.

THE PRESENCE

My wardrobe door will not stay closed these days:
It springs its mirror back into my face like
A parcel I cannot tie; my clothes
Bulge against the panel as the lock gives way
And the door swings softly with the sidelong noise
Of someone entering the room. From my table,
I mark again the fulsome sway
Of garments claiming notice, outfits
Starred in for a night, then hung away, and things
Persistent wear has fashioned to my form. The scent
Of pomander and mothball gives me warning,
One of these days I must air it all, lay them
One by one in order on the bed, to know
Which ones I should get rid of, which to keep, for
As it is, I cannot tell the one from the other, and at night
The wardrobe yawns with the weight it contains,
Watching over my sleep.

PATRICK WILLIAMS

b. 1950

LOST SEED

I found the packets of seed in a cobwebbed drawer.
I can't remember the names now.
Whatever they were, they'd never found the soil.

Your hands were natural with earth.
Earth was a child
Your care drew the best from every year.

Come spring you'd delicately nurse
And every summer our garden
Burned intensely with flowers I couldn't name.

And always you wanted my enthusiasm!
Though I loved them grown,
Sowing and tending bored me, so I ran

Guiltily to other games, you stooped
Settling beds,
Anxiously fathering the frail green.

You should see our garden now, winter or summer.
This bitter November
The front is bleak clumps stuck in mud.

The back is a knee-high tangle
I tried one day to clear with your rusted billhook,
Giving up and going indoors.

We have our different skills.
Not all of life shaped easily in your hands.
Much came twisted or lay sunless and wanting.

Guiltily I absolve our hurt worlds.
Whatever may grow here,
We'll never see the lost seed flower together.

TRAILS

Ten years old with my father
I scoured the rough of the Royal County Down,
I mooched behind a tee as the nobles came
Chatting lightly, four skinny kids
Stumbling after under the weight of the clubs.
I saw my father offer what we'd found
And saw his hand close on the few shillings,
His free hand mock a quick salute:
'Right you are, sir! It's grand weather!'
He'd laugh that night with his peers in the Donard Bar.
Once, shocked, I heard a young man tell him
'Clear off. You're no better than a thief.
Get off the course now or I'll report you.'
I saw my father turn white and turn
As that man teed-up, tensed, swung
Cleanly, smashed the ball out of sight . . .
And my father walked to me with a funny grin.
He said, 'I think we'll head on home now, son.'
And home from scrubbing floors for a lady
My mother dropped breathless into a chair
And lit a cigarette. 'Look in the bag.'
Where under the bread and the spuds and the *Irish News*
Was Rider Haggard or Kipling, once Blake,
Thieved from shelves where she disturbed the dust.

We were afraid some Prod would report her
For earning while my father was unemployed.
Soon I thought our own kind no better,
If anything their weakness sickened more,
Consummate in their role of white negroes.
The sad, lovely songs of wounded Ireland,
Stories of the Tans blown sky-high,
The laughter round the fire turned sour for me.
I left the place where love lay bleeding
But every city where a plane touched down,
Beyond the barrier on every platform,
I limped into one I'd run there from.
Nowhere seemed where I could belong,
I tried to settle but was driven on
When I found that place crowded with the damned.
Where I was was hardly less confusion,
The world a grain of sand whirled where Love
Would never lean to see me move.
Lost on sore trails I turned for home
And here began a reconciliation
With my father's ghost drinking Guinness,
With my mother, rather out of breath.
Secretly I undertook a journey
And understood what I had always known,
Not Teague or Prod or England, Ireland – men
And women trained in ignorance, afraid.
I found myself not lost, not lost completely,
But prisoned where the lock, the key, was me.
At last I turned to you, not knowing you,
I turned to you at last, not trusting you,
Only knowing I would rather die
Free, by you, than die alone in jail.
My trails to us have only just begun
And questions ask one question answers fail,
But if the search is all there is, at least
In you it has a base, almost a home.

RHAPSODY ON MAIN STREET

For the first time since anyone remembers
They've opened the town from one end to the other,
Right from the Donard Bar to the Anchor.
Yellow diggers and men roaring commands
Make more noise and worse than tourist summer,
This year we're cheated of the dead of winter
When even at midday the street is ghostly,
Maybe a disconsolate street cleaner,
A few diehard wives, two cops
Plodding, debating if July is better –
Boozed children with knives in the arcades –
Or this black wind and the one lonely
Offence a frozen dog turd curled on the pavement.
Fortunately I enjoy holes in the ground
And here I can stand and stare at the town's innards,
At pipes spiriting waste and water –
A thousand shithouse doors shyly closing,
The sudden, triumphant flush and Yesterday
Off to be subdued with fierce chemicals –
Sweet water from heaven and the mountains
Into the Silent Valley to our kitchens,
Dousing the burning throats of hungover
Chain-smokers cursing Sunday mornings.
Electricity runs there too
Faster than the water or excrement,
It needs an outlet for its excitement.
This earth is alive and seems friendly,
It seems used to people, to accept
The town on top, so many generations
Have told it something of the human condition.
It's not the heavy shroud of clay inland
But where we walk and send human roots.
One night last week I fell in a trench

And lay back looking at the moon,
Singing snatches of songs as they came.
A passing drunk called, 'Hey! Want a hand?'
'No thanks. I'm fine down here.'
It struck me I wouldn't mind being buried there,
Under the living street and its seasons,
All the voices of July thinning
Through September's casual strollers talking
To quick or faltering steps on a winter's night
And then April and the children running.
I wouldn't be able to see through the tarmacadam
But maybe the roots of the tree in the priests' garden
Would whisper some news of the latest fashions,
The fights on Saturday nights, whose grandson
Was holding hands with whose granddaughter . . .
If the tree died or they cut it down
I'd still be better off than up in Bryansford –
They hear nothing, or now and then
Women weeping, the low voices of men.
In fifty or a hundred years' time
They'd open the street again and find me grinning
Wider than ever living, when I walked
Among them, felt them near, too near, and frowned.

IN THE DARK

They told me God came to Pius
When Pius was worried about the world
And couldn't sleep. I saw that room,
Severe, high-ceilinged, fill with light,
Pius sitting up in the bed
As God stood on the marble floor,
Arms folded, heavily built,

Rugged, old, grave, erect,
Nodding slowly as Pius spoke,
Answering in muted thunder.

Years later in love in bed,
Under you, over you, all along you
Till there was nothing left to do
Only enter you, climbing with you,
Just where we had reached the top
My mind shut against the light –
We were falling, we were sprawled
At the bottom, breathless, sweating.
When you slept I touched your head,
In the dark like Pius praying.

PASSING THROUGH

In me something glimpsed its occasion,
In you something saw not quite
What it wanted. So you smiled, frowning.
So you stayed, leaving, a year.

Sometimes we were good together, then
Asphyxia. In the end I couldn't
Do my tricks to please you, so you sighed.
Crippled conjurer, dumb raconteur.

I wanted you. Wanting you so much
Made certain I'd have less of you less often,
Lose you sooner. No, you're not to blame –
You became another metaphor

For something just beyond me, still untouched,
Teasing through your charms.
But I'll remember. When you left you left
An emptiness. It opens with my arms.

A BABY IN THE HOUSE

She is slim again
And you are on the carpet feeding,
Happy to be dining out.
I watch you follow

My rambling to your father,
Talk of where we've been.
They say how fast you've grown
And now I see you crawl

From strength to strength,
So welcome to the feast
Though soon the walls are gone,
The sky uncertain.

Just watching what you do
And what that does to you
Could tell me all there is to know.
Let me tell your story.

On the bottle too
(It's a celebration)
I'm on my knees to meet you.
Here's looking at you, baby.

ROBERT JOHNSTONE

b. 1951

from NEW INCIDENTS IN THE LIFE OF SHELLEY

II

Not from our dreams, not from our daft cadres
but from somewhere real, the free enclave we
know inside but can't annex, static or

messages are picked up from the tiny
pirate, Radio Shelley. He reads our odes
over the air, sends reports from countries

claiming to be still at peace, where crops grow
and only the facts are changed to protect
our innocence. At his dangerous modes

of thought valves buzz and blush in our old set
on the cleared tea table. Just to have heard
his programme and talk too loud about it

can cost promotion, yet we grab each word.
We demand contact with that better world.

from EVERY CACHE

3

He's a high clear forehead
a debonair moustache
a thornproof jacket
a cardigan that slopes over his belly.

245

Solidly my father
stands eating a plum,
head cocked like a critic
and strikes bargains quickly
with the man in the porkpie hat
who carries a clipboard and agrees
about the quality of goods
under a wall of crates thirty foot high
that's oranges from Haifa
or apples off the freezer trucks
packed in an orchard in France.

Meanwhile I play along a library of palettes.

At the corner of a Cypriot box I see a rotten fruit,
a cushion like a tennis ball of blue blancmange.

There are lemons wrapped in medicated tissues
that have gold pictures of the Venus de Milo.

There are bunches of grapes in barrels full of cork
and you pluck them out like presents from a lucky dip.

There are melons in woodwool like a tray of ostrich eggs
and each callipygous peach has her own safe bed.

The lorries nudge in with inches to spare
among narrow lanes of produce.
All are just painted red,
the merchant's name
three-dimensional.
On the grille of one's
a sprig of white heather
through a polished hubcap
off an American car.

My father deals with the Catholics too.
They've taken their name from their vans
to avoid embarrassment.

I stand in the wooden office
between the spiral stair
and the warm-smelling one-bar fire
and my father takes up so much room
as Ambrose asks me how old I am
before he gives me a carton of mushrooms
shaped like the studs in my father's shirts.

A man in an oilskin apron
stirs a bath full of herring
with a pole encrusted in years of scales.
He takes us to the current sight,
a steely bearded cod
whose tail lollops outside the metal tray.

My father slips past in his low smooth car.
It has chrome strips, extra spotlamps and leather upholstery.

4

Various instants I'm not with you,
waiting at the Heysham boat
before you saw I'd come,
leaning over a fence at the crossroads
of an August evening,

were you thinking of that job you didn't take
in Chicago forty years ago,
or the trawlers parked like dodgems
on our pilgrimage to Aberdeen?

Times you thought I wasn't there
and the sight of you surprised me
I should have used the word 'love'
and didn't.

Opportunities we miss,
moments of each other's lives
we only imagine
help to define us.

But the wonder you took care to teach
for every thing you worked with
was innocent and true.
Like that
we flourish, as we're born to do.

ROBOT CAMERA

When they sent the robot camera down
into the unimaginably null
coldness and darkness of the Atlantic,
hoovering its floor with stadia of light,

and found the uncorroded *Titanic* there
waiting under that tonnage of water,
far down below its heaves and freaks, its clouds
of ice, noumenal, Babylonian,

when they beamed it back, blue-grey, on the box,
it was as if I was seven again,
bathing by the rocks at the Arcadia,
the time I nearly drowned in a breaker

and imagined I understood what death meant –
a breathless, weightless, infantile floating,
a rush of sound, an arm, my own, perhaps,
waving calmly in the mid-foreground

behind the motes and bubbles, sand and salt
particles, minuscule viscosities
migrating all over, aimless as me,
a five-pointed star tumbling in a wave –

how it was not unpleasant except when,
finding myself alive in air once more,
my chest cracked with the pain of the first breath,
the world looked hard, new-washed, indifferent,

compelling as that other silent film
of the whitey-blue, virginal liner,
which looked as if it might mean something more,
had been absorbed into the world of facts,

had made recognisable the face
of an object resembling my father
as the ship's captain, or rather his head
in wax on top of a stuffed uniform,

the expression stiff, the eyes like gross pearls,
saluting posterity for ever,
the third eye of his cap-badge still beaming,
balefully accusing me of life,

and in my nightmare the global current
irresistibly slips me near the wreck
as it remains in white rags of algae
waving on its intact surfaces like

the white hair of an old, honoured person,
and I could be a seal in my black skin,
I look through glass, drift in a bubble-swarm
till I penetrate the slit in the hull

to a space with crushed boxes spilling gold,
its sullen glowing the only life-spark
among the soggy ingots of linen,
a floating comb, tortoiseshell, a mirror,

depthless, colonised, a fountain pen,
then up the full-up, tilted corridors,
liquid as arteries, to the dead heart,
the ballroom, hollow, gaudy as a heart,

where the corpses of the revellers
twirl, bob and turn as perturbing water
jiggles them like a shoal of nervous fish,
fat bodies bursting from their finery

– a bosom overflowing décolletage,
a bull neck strangled by a thin bow tie,
a blimp with shirt-front flapping like a tongue –
then one ruined form floats towards me,

arms outstretched as if to take me dancing
somewhere between ceiling, floors and walls,
and when I push my hand goes through, right through
the tatters of its flesh, the chalky bone,

till it disintegrates in a cloudburst
of cloth and organic stuff comprising
the grey of mother-of-pearl as well as
patches of black and something reddish brown,

but instantly I see my hand swell,
the fingers inflate till the nails lift off,
my putty skin ballooning with a whoosh
and I'm floating again, disconnected,

like an infant, except I seem to know
which way is up, till I wake in a sweat
and reach out to touch the hardness of floor,
the carpet of silt from bed to dresser.

UNDERTAKERS

It's disturbing that it's not a surprise,
to be drawn again towards that problem
lying down there so wonderfully whole
or scattered over the cold calm ocean.

Tonight I sail with the undertakers
out of a smudged newspaper photograph
of Halifax harbour, Nova Scotia.
We've ice, coffins, canvas, tools and chemicals.

The boys with the boat hooks keep plucking up
an awful number of hats, which they set
on deck like streaming molluscs – a top hat,
dunchers, one with ostrich feathers straggling.

A deckchair's now a door into water.
Three dead men in lifebelts lock together
like a snapshot of themselves dancing.
A woman still clings stiffly to a dog.

We identify, embalm, encoffin
all first-class passengers. Second and third

we wrap in canvas. Crew we pack in ice.
A question of time and money, drawing lines,

for even love, or grief, is relative.
Which reminds me – of the bodies laid out
at the Mayflower curling rink, visitors –
relatives – skidding from one to the next,

that poster of the unrecognisable
remains of a person mummified, it seemed,
in the fireblast of the hotel-bombing,
or the fireman gathering limbs in town,

the weeping priest waving his handkerchief,
a crowd of people walking, not running,
in ones and twos away from a cloud of dust.
Oddly, every one has her mouth open.

I dream there are no firemen to clean up
with bin liners. Walk down any street
and you could be in a necropolis,
Warsaw, Leningrad, some maiden city.

The starved or sick lie in their overcoats
like drunkards on the pavement. One walks by.
The van's stopped at the point it hit the child,
the child's body still lies where it landed.

A truck's still toppling a lamp-post, a head
pokes through the windscreen, its face gone missing
like the shop front, blown inside out, rummaged
by a wind into an area of litter.

My mattress is a raft after the wreck,
it bumps through the bodies that bob like mines,

like balloons, like seals standing in water,
uttering their human, repentant cries.

I reach for a victim over the edge
but as my forearms submerge they dissolve,
I tip into the cushion of water,
erasing my face as I slip under.

I'm explaining how stupid this all is,
that I wanted to help, not be rescued,
but my words come out muffled in bubbles
and my lungs are filling like goldfish bags

when up rush two fast boats, one red, one white,
carrying the firemen and the nurse.
He takes his helmet off to look down at me,
she tells me softly to hold out my arms

(which I find I have) and I'm lifted up.
His big raw body kneels to shelter me,
her adolescent body shines with life.
She inoculates me with her selfless love.

EDEN SAYS NO

graffito in Eden village, County Antrim

As a people favoured by the Almighty,
we discovered writing for ourselves
(we've got our own historians, and poets –
some have dubbed us handy with a phrase).
Hence that slogan daubed on the Garden wall.

A reptilian representative
from a firm of nurserymen
(not one of us, if you catch my meaning)
tried to induce us to turn commercial
with free samples of edible fruit
and all types of honeyed talk.

But we know what we've got in Eden
and we aren't about to throw it away.
The slogan reminds us, as much as them,
that our soil must stay pure and unsullied.
Within these walls fruit shall never grow
because Eden will always say No.

THE FRUIT OF KNOWLEDGE

In a wee, twee cul-de-sac
beside Kilroot
entitled the Garden of Eden,
a man on a kitchen chair
has placed himself in the sun
among grandchildren.

   The last image of my dad
   was in the rear-view mirror
   of the car he'd given me,
   my father and mother
   on the Lisburn Road,
   waving as I left for England.

   But his hand raised
   wishing good luck
   also played an invisible line
   to a fish tearing a hook:

254

in High Street now and Royal Avenue
I hear the waters under my feet.

    Someday, to release the world
    from the memory of what we were,
    the wave of the past,
    the wave of history,
    will drown grave, field and thoroughfare
    from the Garden of Eden to Edenderry.

PAUL MULDOON

b. 1951

THE FIELD HOSPITAL

Taking, giving back their lives
By the strength of our bare hands,
By the silence of our knives,
We answer to no grey South

Nor blue North, not self-defence,
The lie of just wars, neither
Cold nor hot blood's difference
In their discharging of guns,

But that hillside of fresh graves.
Would this girl brought to our tents
From whose flesh we have removed
Shot that George, on his day off,

Will use to weight fishing lines,
Who died screaming for ether,
Yet protest our innocence?
George lit the lanterns, in danced

Those gigantic yellow moths
That brushed right over her wounds,
Pinning themselves to our sleeves
Like medals given the brave.

THE MIXED MARRIAGE

My father was a servant boy.
When he left school at eight or nine
He took up billhook and loy
To win the ground he would never own.

My mother was the schoolmistress,
The world of Castor and Pollux.
There were twins in her own class.
She could never tell which was which.

She had read one volume of Proust,
He knew the cure for farcy.
I flitted between a hole in the hedge
And a room in the Latin Quarter.

When she had cleared the supper table
She opened *The Acts of the Apostles*,
Aesop's Fables, Gulliver's Travels.
Then my mother went on upstairs

And my father further dimmed the light
To get back to hunting with ferrets
Or the factions of the faction-fights,
The Ribbon Boys, the Caravats.

MA

Old photographs would have her bookish, sitting
Under a willow. I take that to be a croquet
Lawn. She reads aloud, no doubt from Rupert Brooke.
The month is always May or June.

Or with the stranger on the motorbike.
Not my father, no. This one's all crew-cut
And polished brass buttons.
An American soldier, perhaps.
                              And the full moon
Swaying over Keenaghan, the orchards and the cannery,
Thins to a last yellow-hammer, and goes.
The neighbours gather, all Keenaghan and Collegelands,
There is storytelling. Old miners at Coalisland
Going into the ground. Swinging, for fear of the gas,
The soft flame of a canary.

CUBA

My eldest sister arrived home that morning
In her white muslin evening dress.
'Who the hell do you think you are,
Running out to dances in next to nothing?
As though we hadn't enough bother
With the world at war, if not at an end.'
My father was pounding the breakfast table.

'Those Yankees were touch and go as it was –
If you'd heard Patton in Armagh –
But this Kennedy's nearly an Irishman
So he's not much better than ourselves.
And him with only to say the word.
If you've got anything on your mind
Maybe you should make your peace with God.'

I could hear May from beyond the curtain.
'Bless me, Father, for I have sinned.
I told a lie once, I was disobedient once.

And, Father, a boy touched me once.'
'Tell me, child. Was this touch immodest?
Did he touch your breast, for example?'
'He brushed against me, Father. Very gently.'

ANSEO

When the Master was calling the roll
At the primary school in Collegelands,
You were meant to call back *Anseo*
And raise your hand
As your name occurred.
Anseo, meaning here, here and now,
All present and correct,
Was the first word of Irish I spoke.
The last name on the ledger
Belonged to Joseph Mary Plunkett Ward
And was followed, as often as not,
By silence, knowing looks,
A nod and a wink, the Master's droll
'And where's our little Ward-of-court?'

I remember the first time he came back
The Master had sent him out
Along the hedges
To weigh up for himself and cut
A stick with which he would be beaten.
After a while, nothing was spoken;
He would arrive as a matter of course
With an ash-plant, a salley-rod.
Or, finally, the hazel-wand
He had whittled down to a whip-lash,
Its twist of red and yellow lacquers

Sanded and polished,
And altogether so delicately wrought
That he had engraved his initials on it.

I last met Joseph Mary Plunkett Ward
In a pub just over the Irish border.
He was living in the open,
In a secret camp
On the other side of the mountain.
He was fighting for Ireland,
Making things happen.
And he told me, Joe Ward,
Of how he had risen through the ranks
To Quartermaster, Commandant:
How every morning at parade
His volunteers would call back *Anseo*
And raise their hands
As their names occurred.

THE WEEPIES

Most Saturday afternoons
At the local Hippodrome
Saw the Pathé-News rooster,
Then the recurring dream

Of a lonesome drifter
Through uninterrupted range.
Will Hunter, so gifted
He could peel an orange

In a single, fluent gesture,
Was the leader of our gang.

260

The curtain rose this afternoon
On a lion, not a gong.

When the crippled girl
Who wanted to be a dancer
Met the married man
Who was dying of cancer,

Our hankies unfurled
Like flags of surrender.
I believe something fell asunder
In even Will Hunter's hands.

TRUCE

It begins with one or two soldiers
And one or two following
With hampers over their shoulders.
They might be off wildfowling

As they would another Christmas Day,
So gingerly they pick their steps.
No one seems sure of what to do.
All stop when one stops.

A fire gets lit. Some spread
Their greatcoats on the frozen ground.
Polish vodka, fruit and bread
Are broken out and passed round.

The air of an old German song,
The rules of Patience, are the secrets
They'll share before long.
They draw on their last cigarettes

As Friday-night lovers, when it's over,
Might get up from their mattresses
To congratulate each other
And exchange names and addresses.

QUOOF

How often have I carried our family word
for the hot water bottle
to a strange bed,
as my father would juggle a red-hot half-brick
in an old sock
to his childhood settle.
I have taken it into so many lovely heads
or laid it between us like a sword.

A hotel room in New York City
with a girl who spoke hardly any English,
my hand on her breast
like the smouldering one-off spoor of the yeti
or some other shy beast
that has yet to enter the language.

GATHERING MUSHROOMS

The rain comes flapping through the yard
like a tablecloth that she hand-embroidered.
My mother has left it on the line.
It is sodden with rain.
The mushroom shed is windowless, wide,
its high-stacked wooden trays
hosed down with formaldehyde.

And my father has opened the Gates of Troy
to that first load of horse manure.
Barley straw. Gypsum. Dried blood. Ammonia.
Wagon after wagon
blusters in, a self-renewing gold-black dragon
we push to the back of the mind.
We have taken our pitchforks to the wind.

All brought back to me that September evening
fifteen years on. The pair of us
tripping through Barnett's fair demesne
like girls in long dresses
after a hail-storm.
We might have been thinking of the fire-bomb
that sent Malone House sky-high
and its priceless collection of linen
sky-high.
We might have wept with Elizabeth McCrum.
We were thinking only of psilocybin.
You sang of the maid you met on the dewy grass –
And she stooped so low gave me to know
it was mushrooms she was gathering O.

He'll be wearing that same old donkey jacket
and the sawn-off waders.
He carries a knife, two punnets, a bucket.
He reaches far into his own shadow.
We'll have taken him unawares
and stand behind him, slightly to one side.
He is one of those ancient warriors
before the rising tide.
He'll glance back from under his peaked cap
without breaking rhythm:
his coaxing a mushroom – a flat or a cup –
the nick against his right thumb;

the bucket then, the punnet to left or right,
and so on and so forth till kingdom come.
We followed the overgrown towpath by the Lagan.
The sunset would deepen through cinnamon
to aubergine,
the wood pigeon's concerto for oboe and strings,
allegro, blowing your mind.
And you were suddenly out of my ken, hurtling
towards the ever-receding ground,
into the maw
of a shimmering green-gold dragon.
You discovered yourself in some outbuilding
with your long-lost companion, me,
though my head had grown into the head of a horse
that shook its dirty-fair mane
and spoke this verse.

Come back to us. However cold and raw, your feet
were always meant
to negotiate terms with bare cement.
Beyond this concrete wall is a wall of concrete
and barbed wire. Your only hope
is to come back. If sing you must, let your song
tell of treading your own dung,
let straw and dung give a spring to your step.
If we never live to see the day we leap
into our true domain,
lie down with us now and wrap
yourself in the soiled grey blanket of Irish rain
that will, one day, bleach itself white.
Lie down with us and wait.

AISLING

I was making my way home late one night
this summer, when I staggered
into a snow drift.

Her eyes spoke of a sloe-year,
her mouth a year of haws.

Was she Aurora, or the goddess Flora,
Artemidora, or Venus bright,
or Anorexia, who left
a lemon stain on my flannel sheet?

It's all much of a muchness.

In Belfast's Royal Victoria Hospital
a kidney machine
supports the latest hunger striker
to have called off his fast, a saline
drip into his bag of brine.

A lick and a promise. Cuckoo spittle.
I hand my sample to Doctor Maw.
She gives me back a confident *All Clear*.

MEETING THE BRITISH

We met the British in the dead of winter.
The sky was lavender

and the snow lavender-blue.
I could hear, far below,

the sound of two streams coming together
(both were frozen over)

and, no less strange,
myself calling out in French

across that forest-
clearing. Neither General Jeffrey Amherst

nor Colonel Henry Bouquet
could stomach our willow-tobacco.

As for the unusual
scent when the Colonel shook out his hand-

kerchief: *C'est la lavande,
une fleur mauve comme le ciel.*

They gave us six fishhooks
and two blankets embroidered with smallpox.

GERALD DAWE

b. 1952

NAMES

They call this 'Black North'
black from the heart out –

it doesn't matter about
particularities when mouths

mumble the handy sayings
and day-in minds tighten.

I've been here having thought
nowhere else was possible,

a condition of destiny or what
the old generations only fumbled

with: conceit, success, a fair
share of decent hardship,

compounded, forced into fierce
recognition – the cardhouse toppled.

In this extreme, perched
on the edge of the Atlantic

you feel to look down
and gather around the details

thinking to store them away
bundle and pack in the exile's way –

the faithful journey
of turning your back

like the host of others
the scholars and saints.

Line up and through the turn-
stile, click the ticket

and wait till you're
clear of it: glued to

the passport: IRISH POET,
Destination, America or

Early Grave. You need never
recall the other names.

SHELTERING PLACES

for Norma Fitzgerald

It's been pelting down
all night the kind
of rain that drenches
to the bone

and a dirtstorm
in the carpark.
The hot wind carries
thunder making girls

scream and old men
count the seconds,

improvising distance
as you shout to

turn the lights out
pull down the blinds
so that lightning can't
get in and frazzle us up

in the curtain-dark room
the rumbles near and
shattering flashes
make everything go numb.

The storm is reaching
home territory, stretching
over the hills down
into our sheltering places.

A QUESTION OF COVENANTS

28 September 1913

The *Patriotic* turns to face
an invisible sea. From Castle Place
thousands swarm through side streets
and along the unprotected quays just
to glimpse Carson, gaunt as usual,
who watches the surge of people
call, *'Don't leave us. You mustn't leave us'*,
and in the searchlight's beam,
his figure arched across the upper deck,
he shouts he will come back
and, if necessary, fight this time.

It is what they came to hear
in the dark September night.
As the *Patriotic* sails out
Union colours burst in rockets
and bonfires scar the hills
he departs from, a stranger to both sides
of the lough's widening mouth
and the crowd's distant singing
'Auld Lang Syne' and 'God Save the King'.

SEAMEN'S MISSION

The high dome
sticks out in my mind
as the minister kneads
the pulpit's bow

ferrying us through
treacherous oceans.
Outside the sun dabbles
and in the beams

of stained glass dust
radiates from nowhere
to the vaulted dreams
of our departed, heads

uplifted under royal
flags and conquering
psalms of the spirit.
The girls fidget

and elders adjust
themselves for the final

270

half-hour. Let
the bells ring out:

we who praise Hope
will stand together
in stone-cold portals
blinking with the light.

SOLSTICE

for my daughter

You arrived that bad winter
when I was like a man
walking in a circle no one else was near.

The lakes behind had frozen,
from the dump gulls came and went
and the news was all discontent,

of *Sell-out* and blame for the dead
country-boy faces that already were
fading from church wall and gate,

but the seas tightened their grip
when you faced the light and let rip
a first cry of bewilderment

at this beginning, the snow
buttressed against brilliant windows,
and where they washed you clean

I saw the ice outside fall
and imagined the fires burning
on the Hill of Tara ring

across the concealed earth
towards a silent hospital
and our standing still

all around you, Olwen,
transfixed by your birth
in such a bitter season.

THE LIKELIHOOD OF SNOW/THE DANGER OF FIRE

Around five in the next garden, a rooster
starts up his rusty banter and the first flight,
coast to coast , soars through an endless sky.
We are hatching in the bedroom downstairs
our special dreams, maybe of home, who knows? –
heads together, facing, I suppose, the sun,
which has left you to this evening's viewing,
with a good fire down and the curtains drawn
on shining streets and the likelihood of snow.
Sprinklers will soon play across impeccable lawns
and the puppetry of emblazoned butterflies begins
with air conditioning, humming like a ship's engines,
while the two imperious cockatoos
take to the surrounding suburban trees.

I've been asking myself, head crooked in arms,
why it could be so easy to forget about home
and all the mumbo-jumbo about one's *People*.
'Mine', if such they are, look for all the world

like great Deniers, the staunch, unflappable self-
deceit of always seeming to be in the right
and the fear of being found out that they are not.
I have watched since childhood their marches and parades,
with banners aloft, swords and bibles displayed,
and I have passed the banks of clipped hedges, the front rooms
with oval mirrors and cabinets full of photographs –
the husband in the Army, son in the Boys' Brigade,
a fallen brother, the Royal Wedding –
and never known my *People* since they kept
to themselves in desperate innocence,
or persist behind transparent walls to explode in hate,
or, like me in another hemisphere,
they disappear in dreams:
as stewards on ocean-going liners,
managers of building societies,
multinational executives,
further up or down the scale of things,
the accents mellow to a faint American twang
or a touch of the Anglo-
we to whom no surface is deep enough
grin and bear the nonchalant enquiry,
'Where do you come from?'
and know that the only real news here today
is the danger of fire.

CANBERRA

WILLIAM PESKETT

b. 1952

THE QUESTION OF TIME

Where on earth
has the stumbling mammoth gone?
that giant tripper over nations
who used to think
the world was his
after the succulent brontosaurus.

The ages shed no tears for me.
I am not their resting
but their passing through,
left to watch
the intricate bees
in their noble art of dance.

STAR AND SEA

That star I now see
blended in the night's bright telegraph
has long since burnt out
and exploded.
The slowness of its fumes of light
across space provides
a second's vision of the past.
Gleeful time-traveller,
I forget I'm divided from a truth.

Cold water from the south
melts sombre
from the brilliant cap.
The slow currents north
take seven years to chill me,
to reach me with their dated clutter
from the ocean floor – time enough
for sea-change, a skin-change;
a new man reading old news.

THE INHERITORS

for Paul Muldoon

And the ones that got tough
ripped the soft parts
from the sea.
With a spine and a jaw
they pressed a clear advantage,
picking bones with ones
whose shadows met their own.
Gasping, they broke the surface.

The ones that had legs
came up where there was nothing.
Starting as one,
they split into bands
and savaged the green ground.
Ambivalent, they slid in the swamp
from home to home, cleverer,
keeping their options open.

The ones that could crawl
stood up and dried

the afterbirth from their backs.
Somehow they grew to break
the treaty of the land:
becoming gross they tore
the flesh of the sinless
and took three elements in their stride.

The ones that were feathered
came to know the slaughter
of the plain. Gliding from cliffs
they tumbled to the line of flight.
Innocent in the air, their shapes
against the sun began to drop –
below, their claws ripped fur
from nervous carcasses.

And the ones that gave suck
ran like warm blood
through high branches.
With a crib for their young
their lives might have been maternal
but for precedent. Not born
to run with the innocent,
inheritors, we kill.

BOTTLES IN THE ZOOLOGICAL MUSEUM

Bottles are for sleeping in –
they exorcise you
giving a live and pink
fluorescence to your skin.

Bottles contain you,
sinless and dreamless

you sink in their liquid
as eiderdown.

There are never men
in bottles – only animals
and babies and half-babies,
their softness gritting.

No man is accepted here.
I see a foetus crouch,
not in attack
but discovery of other shelves.

WINDOW DRESSING

The beautiful man and his wife
must have fled,
deserting their immaculate husks
like wholesome insects
on a jagged flight to a new life.

The copies that remain possess everything.
In their still and vigilant life
of display they need cocktail cabinets
and sofas
but have no inclination to move over,

to touch and merge.
The actual people, lush and naked,
are hovering on transient wings:
they're making love
out of hours.

On dark nights, through the window
on their brilliant home
I see them returning,
sheepish and ashamed,
slipping back into shape.

FROM BELFAST TO SUFFOLK

First the pleasures fire the heart –
sutures of oak and elm
divide acres of polyploid grasses
into skull plates
to civilise every corner of the country.
Driving from the Low House
we might pass a dozen churches,
towers that indicate
walking distance across the fields
set alight with beacons.

More honest than the view from innocence
where plumes of smoke along the skyline
describe another operation,
here, the factory workers of the earth
are burning stubble,
purifying the season.
Later, driving tractors in the dark
the sharp spotlight turns
a glistening edge of soil
in long tracks across the land.

The night-police don't scare me here.
Like the man who, in the end,
neglects his mother for his wife

a faithfulness supersedes
the pleasures of the moon.
This demilitarised home
protects me like the other –
its signpost names pronounceable,
its fields the map
in my head.

ANDREW ELLIOTT

b. 1961

THE STAY BEHIND

Now that the men have gone off to the choleric wars,
Writing letters to their families, glimpses of themselves
In the stinking trenches or the infra-red streets,
The writing flexing like barbed wire in their minds,
Or the veins which appear in lint swabs held to a wound –

I am like the sick child who takes the day off school
To stay at home among feminine things –
You cracking eggs into a speckled chipped bowl –
Remembering how on the shelf in the bathroom
There is a new jar of moisturising cream for your skin.

THE LOVE POEM

In bed with our bodies so completely intertwined
That we have both lost touch with our limbs –
As if our flesh and bones have dissolved into one
Relaxing creature – and with your cried-out eyes
No more than inches from my dry eyes I know

What it is makes you content is the thought
Of never again being lonely. So, letting our temples
Touch, I put my head to yours and instantly
It is as if a shutter has opened into the film show
In my mind and I've been caught in the act

Of dreaming all the others that there could be,
Their perfect bodies lying back and open in the grass

They've flattened and embroidered with flowers
Or in their lamp-lit, peach-pink rooms,
Letting their dresses slip off their shoulders . . .

Me – so full of it all and so easily led astray
That in the end I learn quite quickly the way to
Steel myself against your eyes in the dark – already writing
The first perfect line of the one perfect poem she'll inspire:
In bed with our bodies so completely intertwined.

THE X-RAY

Disentangling our lives –
sorting out our things
into who owns what
and what goes where,

like the separating
of our underthings
into two neat piles
from the jumble

of the cupboard
or the drawer –
would be easy
but for our child,

a little girl or boy
who between us
floats unconceived
and dreamed of

like the last egg
going slowly cold

in a nest abandoned
but still cradled in the
branches of two entangled

crackling trees.

ANGEL

I think to make love to a nurse would be perfect,
Every germ and virus swimming in her mind
Like a kaleidoscope moving

Under a patient's skin,
Her breasts having nightmares of cancer,
Her hands like bowls weighing the ghosts of diseases.

Because she cannot control what she sees
Her body has turned inside out in the way she talks,
And left me, like a willing unfortunate,

To make my love nest
Among imaginary glands
And strange passageways,

The pink and white tissues of her genitals;
Unvaccinated and tempting fate
By bedding down with the untouchables,

Loving everything that happens under her skin.

HERE TODAY . . .

Making love down through the centuries
Men have left their shadow on women.

Nowadays I want the shadow I leave
To be that of a bird on the bed of a stream.

JOHN HUGHES

b. 1962

DOG DAY LESSON

Savouring the shade of our teacher's willow
we read of Hannibal crossing the Alps –
how his leisurely elephants laid tracks
the ice holds to this day.
Then there was the razing of Carthage,
an empire's salt sown among its rubble
in the hope of baiting the sea.
We learnt that in its time
the world knew it as the city of glass,
the place of perfect symmetries,
with gardens laid by legions of glass-men
whose every breath could form
quivering chandeliers of trees.
There the people lived as faith healers,
curing by crystallising all they touched,
giving and taking a perfection to their lives.

KNOWINGNESS

The well-dressed couple haggle
over the price of pleasure,
oblivious of the twelve-year-old boy
who has wandered in off the street
to sell the local newspaper;
he listens to their carnal business
with a kind of knowingness
I find not a little frightening.

When they finally do notice him
they settle everything with a smirk
and walk out of the restaurant
without having eaten a bite.
In time the boy offers me a cigarette
and lists room numbers
where that couple may or may not be
entering the realms of make-believe.

A RESPECT FOR LAW AND ORDER

for Dermot Seymour

The general will be shot in the face
when his new chauffeur forgets orders
and stops for a red traffic light.
Within the hour one of the usual suspects
will be rounded up and taken downtown
to an interrogation room on the tenth floor
of the National Central Security building;
and after five hours of electric shocks
and beatings with a length of rubber hose
he will be ordered to open the window
and step outside for a breath of fresh air.

He will fall head-first onto a crowded pavement
of journalists, pickpockets, private detectives,
air-force pilots, French polishers, jazz-guitarists,
civil servants in the Department of Information,
elderly women on their way across town
to visit their latest grandchild,
young men sauntering to a soccer match
between the national side and Paraguay,
a famous Italian new expressionist painter,

285

and the newly arrived cultural attaché
of the Republic of South Africa.

The suspect will then pick himself up,
take a look at himself in the nearest window,
tuck in his shirt, straighten his tie,
and disappear into the leafy suburb
where he lives in a modest apartment
with his second wife and her two children;
and finish the book he was reading
when interrupted by an old school friend
dressed to the nines in a uniform
he had recently come to respect.

PETER MCDONALD

b. 1962

PLEASURES OF THE IMAGINATION

Again I'm caught staring
at the sky, in particular
those blue-black clouds
that shadow the sun. I remember
I was meant for a painter
and see in a puddle
cause for reflection.

I've packed my bags again
for cloud-cuckoo-land;
you might see me there,
mouth agape, as I recline
on beds of asphodel,
finally reaping the benefits
of a classical education.

But there are other approaches;
the celebrated Donal O'Sheugh
owes his allegiance
to a different culture.
He has carpeted his apartment
in the heart of New Jersey
with the best Irish turf

(perhaps, all the time,
he was speaking in parables).
Not that it matters –
I think I could stay here
amazed by this September

sun-shower, quite silent,
until his cows come home.

Meanwhile, on a deserted
filmset, the handsome
Count Dracula has heard tell
that he is a metaphor now,
and is unhappy.
He aspires to symbolism
and perhaps, one day, to nothing at all.

CHRISTMAS

The spaceship drifting up
from the ground to the second floor
of the Belfast Co-op
to ferry me and a dozen others

into the presence, slides home
and unloads me, while
my tight frown fixes
each request exactly

for him to hear and remember.
He takes me on his knee
and offers, to go on with,
a yellow plastic steamship.

Later it occurs to me
that somehow he is able
to appear in more
than one place at a time,

for he suffers the little children
in five or six stores daily.
But in mysteries like this
everything is possible:

him riding in the air
through a night speckled
with snow-fluff, or Michelin
spacemen in orbit,

their cracked despatches
indecipherable; even the child
my mother never had, waking
early on Christmas morning,

who finds his presents waiting
at the foot of the bed
exactly as he dreamt them,
and begins to smile.

CASH POSITIVE

Two telephones all morning giving each other hell
in the highest office between here and God,
a desk polished black so you can see your face
and a silent screen that flashes messages

across cities, oceans and thousands of miles;
a printer beside it zipping away, murmuring
at intervals all day in different inks;
nobody says much except to the telephones.

I'd start by talking about securities,
though nobody is ever safe, and things

get sticky, dangerous – you might even
pick up something nasty from the keyboard

or the one love of your life, just think of that.
And what reply *is* there anyway
to the fax's cruel jibing, its clever *This*
is the promised land calling, the poor boy on the line?

TOTALLED

The costumes are a kind of late-colonial,
all primary colours and designer labels;
the hair's worn long and blow-dried, accents
are halfway between here and America;
a badge on his lapel says the producer
won't take no for an answer, and maybe
it's true he has a way with the impossible:
resprayed old cars, given a last polish,
catapult into walls and shop windows,
into each other, they're always totalled,
and right on cue the flames come bursting
just to make everything final;
the sound's dubbed later, of fists connecting,
gunshots, brakes, happy or sad music.

Two men are waiting in a skyline office,
each one silently adding up the other
and playing the razor-cool executive.
The first smoothes a map, points to one corner,
and thinks out all the disadvantages –
it's too late, and impossible anyway,
to make much of that sector. He's starting
to speak now, with a shrug in his voice
and his eyes fixed on the middle distance,

part of him slipping out to some margin
as a young achiever jokes in a monotone
of how already he's allowed for losses
and nowadays, in any case, that country
is washed-up, written-off, a place for dead people.

SUNDAY IN GREAT TEW

8th November 1987

1

It's time to get back to the car. Already, at half-past three,
the light's three-quarters gone, and back across the green
you can watch the shifting greys of a subtle fog by now
coming over to freeze the steps we leave, our ghosts' footprints,

to slight marks in November grass, and that's the last
of us this afternoon, this year, in this model village
a half-hour's drive from Oxford, where we come in summer
like the other tourists, to drink decent beer, sniff woodsmoke,

and admire thatched roofs on sturdy, stone-built houses,
as though the whole place were a replica of some England,
an idea on show, unchanging, glassy, not quite touchable.
But this is November, and Sunday. It is Sunday in Great Tew.

2

Every visit nowadays is an act of remembrance,
measuring changes in us against some other summer
when we sat here drinking, and swapped our random gossip
– friends, work and books, hard politics or love –

across a wooden table in an always busy pub
with proper beer on sale, not the watery Oxford slops,
and where, as their speciality, they sell handmade pipes,
briars and clay pipes, every one the genuine article

(though these, admittedly, we never got around to buying);
one year we're talking about that headstrong, happy girl
you'd chased unluckily for months; another, and we're
    discussing
far-off acts of war, the real thing, here in the Falkland Arms.

3

The manor house, concealed behind thick trees and hedges,
might well be home now for some eccentric millionaire
who seldom shows his face; from the road going uphill
to the church, you can see through gaps down to the house
    itself,

heavy and strong, like the brash history it suggests,
having and holding so much; was it here since the Civil War,
when the bookish man who owned the place, Lord Falkland,
was a loyalist who found himself outmanoeuvred?

Once he played patron here to the poet Abraham Cowley
– outmanoeuvred himself, in his way, by Parliament's
staunch worker Milton, true to different lights, but blind,
po-faced, pig-headed and holy, almost an Ulsterman.

4

Names of the wars change, and of course the protagonists
    change:
the church contains its various slabs of memorial stone
with names of the dead men, where today a single wreath
of poppies does its duty, pays them its stiff homage

of glaring red flowers for death, rootless and papery,
bunched together in grief or pride, or with indifference,
on a Sunday like any other Sunday in November;
there's a smell of damp mixed with the smell of genteel ladies

and the cold slips forward from the walls and the dark floor
so that here, too, we must become aliens, shut out
from whatever we might be tempted to call our own, reminded
that the dead are close, that here the poppy is an English flower.

5

There are no words to find for the dead, and no gestures,
no sermons to be turned, no curses to lay now and for ever
on one house, or the other, or on both; there is no need
to rerun the scalding images they have left in our keeping,

or pitch hot misery into this cold comfort, as though
one ill-bred outburst here might make sense of it;
there is no need to watch television in the afternoon
to understand that nobody has ever died with a good reason,

and see the Irish slaughter one another like wogs;
there is no need, only now a blinding appetite,
this afternoon, tomorrow, the day after; so tonight in the
    Killyhevlin
Hotel the team from ITN will be ordering champagne.

6

One drink today, one pint of beer, and one short walk
in the sober afternoon around an English village,
a conversation jumping from one silence to another
in ripe Oxonian vowels, two figures on their own

in some pretend backwater with picture-postcard views,
slipping discreetly into a proper country churchyard
and quoting poetry, and laughing now that everything's
too late, imagining the right history for the place,

inglorious, largely mute: two generals discussing terms,
their fists set hard on the oak table that's between them,
where neither will say the word 'defeat', though both return
with different names for victory to their beaten people.

7

Even in the middle of winter, the sky is everywhere,
folded above us as we walk with hands sunk in our pockets,
our fingers worrying over cold coins and key-rings;
it covers us completely as a numbing anaesthetic

so that every time we might look up, the two of us,
the trees we can see with fog trailing in their branches,
the scarecrow standing up in its one blank field
(or what looks from here like a scarecrow), the row of old houses

snug and expensive and empty, even the pub behind us,
all become incidental, oblique marks set in the margin,
swept out to the edges of a single, clear perspective,
the one that matters most, or least, and never changes.

8

A flower of crumpled paper with its button of black plastic
has fallen from somebody's coat, and is lying here beside
a vacant phone box opposite the village school
along with an empty packet of twenty Benson and Hedges

and what looks like a bus ticket; such modest litter
might be the last thing you notice, and for all the cars parked

there's nobody here but us walking out in the open,
and even we are making our way back to a car,

opening, closing doors, clicking in seat belts, switching on
dipped headlights and starting the engine, turning around
and taking a right at the deserted school,
on our way home, leaving absolutely nothing behind us.

BIOGRAPHICAL
AND
BIBLIOGRAPHICAL
NOTES

GEORGE BUCHANAN

b. 1904 in Kilwaughter, Larne, County Antrim, d. 1989. Educated Larne Grammar School and Campbell College, Belfast. Worked as a journalist on various Irish and English newspapers, including *The Times*. Joined RAF in 1940. Chairman, Town and Country Development Committee, NI, 1949–53. In addition to his collections of poems, he has published two journals: *Passage through the Present* (1932) and *Words for Tonight* (1936); six novels: *A London Story* (1935), *Rose Forbes* (Part I, 1937, Parts I and II, 1950), *Entanglement* (1938), *The Soldier and the Girl* (1940), *A Place to Live* (1952) and *Naked Reason* (1971); two volumes of autobiography: *Green Seacoast* (1959) and *Morning Papers* (1965); and a volume of essays: *The Politics of Culture* (1977). His plays *Dance Night* (1934), *A Trip to the Castle* (1960) and *Tresper Revolution* (1961) were all staged in London.

POETRY COLLECTIONS BY GEORGE BUCHANAN

Bodily Responses, Gaberbocchus, 1958
Conversation with Strangers, Gaberbocchus, 1961
Annotations, Carcanet Press, 1970
Minute-Book of a City, Carcanet Press, 1972
Inside Traffic, Carcanet Press, 1976
Possible Being, Carcanet Press, 1980
Adjacent Columns, Menard Press/Carcanet Press, 1982

ABOUT GEORGE BUCHANAN

'George Buchanan: a special supplement', *Honest Ulsterman*, no. 59 (March/June, 1978), pp. 17–87

RECORDING

George Buchanan Reading his Poems, cassette, Audio Arts, London, 1977

CIARAN CARSON

b. 1948 in Belfast. Educated at St Mary's CBS and Queen's University Belfast. Won an Eric Gregory Award for poetry in 1978 and the Alice Hunt Bartlett Award of the Poetry Society in 1987. He works as Traditional Arts Officer with the Arts Council of Northern Ireland and his *Pocket Guide to Irish Traditional Music* was published by Appletree Press in 1986.

POETRY COLLECTIONS BY CIARAN CARSON

The New Estate, Blackstaff Press, 1976
The Irish for No, Gallery Press/Bloodaxe Books, 1987
The New Estate and Other Poems, Gallery Press, 1988
Belfast Confetti, Gallery Press/Bloodaxe Books, 1989

ABOUT CIARAN CARSON

Brandes, Rand (interviewer). 'Ciaran Carson', *Irish Review*, no. 8
   (Spring 1990), pp. 77–90

GERALD DAWE

b. 1952 in Belfast. Educated at Orangefield Boys' School, the New
University of Ulster, and University College Galway, where he was
awarded an MA in 1978. Lecturer at University College Galway and,
currently, Trinity College Dublin. Has received a Major State Award for
research (1974–7), an Arts Council Bursary for poetry (1980) and the
Macauley Fellowship for Literature (1984). Edited the anthology *The
Younger Irish Poets* (Blackstaff Press, 1982; new edition, forthcoming,
1991) and co-edited, with Edna Longley, the collection of essays *Across
a Roaring Hill: The Protestant Imagination in Modern Ireland* (Blackstaff
Press, 1985). He founded the magazine *Krino* in 1986 and has edited it
since then.

POETRY COLLECTIONS BY GERALD DAWE

Sheltering Places, Blackstaff Press, 1978
The Lundys Letter, Gallery Press, 1985
Sunday School, Gallery Press, 1990

SEAMUS DEANE

b. 1940 in Derry. Educated at St Columb's College, Derry, Queen's
University Belfast and Cambridge University. He has taught at Reed
College, Notre Dame, and the University of California at Berkeley and
is now Professor of Modern English and American Literature at Uni-
versity College Dublin. His first collection of poems, *Gradual Wars*, won
the AE Memorial Award. In addition to poetry, he has published the
critical studies *Celtic Revivals: Essays in Modern Irish Literature 1880–
1980* (Faber and Faber, 1985) and *A Short History of Irish Literature*
(Hutchinson, 1986). Co-edited the periodicals *Atlantis* and the *Crane Bag*

and is a founder-member of the Field Day Theatre Company. General editor (Andrew Carpenter, associate editor) of *The Field Day Anthology of Irish Writing, c. 550–1990*, 3 vols, Field Day, forthcoming, 1991. His novel *Reading in the Dark* will be published by Granta/Penguin in 1991.

POETRY COLLECTIONS BY SEAMUS DEANE

Gradual Wars, Irish University Press, 1972
Rumours, Dolmen Press, 1977
History Lessons, Gallery Press, 1983
Selected Poems, Gallery Press, 1988

ANDREW ELLIOTT

b. 1961 in Limavady, County Derry. Spent early childhood in Banbridge, County Down, and attended Coleraine Academical Institution as boarder. Studied for a year in Cardiff, then at Queen's University Belfast, from where he graduated in 1984. In 1985 he was the first recipient of the Allan Dowling Poetry Travelling Fellowship, which he used for a year's sojourn in the USA. A selection of his poems was included in the anthology *Trio Poetry 4* (Blackstaff Press, 1985).

POETRY COLLECTION BY ANDREW ELLIOTT

The Creationists, Blackstaff Press, 1988

PADRAIC FIACC

b. 1924 in Belfast. Family emigrated to New York, where Fiacc was educated at Commerce and Haaren High Schools, Manhattan, and St Joseph's Seminary, Calicoon, New York State. Returned to Belfast in 1936. Won the AE Memorial Award in 1947. Edited *The Wearing of the Black* (Blackstaff Press, 1974), an anthology of poems about the Troubles.

POETRY COLLECTIONS BY PADRAIC FIACC

By the Black Stream, Dolmen Press, 1969
Odour of Blood, Goldsmith Press, 1973
Nights in the Bad Place, Blackstaff Press, 1977
The Selected Padraic Fiacc, Blackstaff Press, 1979
Missa Terribilis, Blackstaff Press, 1986

ABOUT PADRAIC FIACC

Brown, Terence. 'Padraic Fiacc: the bleeding bough', in *Northern Voices: Poets from Ulster*, Gill and Macmillan, 1975, pp. 141–8

Dawe, Gerald. 'Secret being: the poetry of Padraic Fiacc', *Honest Ulsterman*, no. 67 (October 1980–February 1981), pp. 71–82

Longley, Edna. Introduction to *The Selected Padraic Fiacc*, Blackstaff Press, 1979

MICHAEL FOLEY

b. 1947 in Derry. Educated at St Columb's College, Derry, and Queen's University Belfast, where he took a degree in chemistry and did research in computer science. Joint-edited the *Honest Ulsterman* (with Frank Ormsby), 1969–72. His novel, *The Life of Jamesie Coyle*, was serialised in *Fortnight* magazine in 1978 and issued by Fortnight Publications in 1984. Now lectures in computer science at the Polytechnic of Central London.

POETRY COLLECTIONS BY MICHAEL FOLEY

True Life Love Stories, Blackstaff Press, 1976
The Irish Frog: Versions of Laforgue, Ulsterman Publications, 1978
The GO Situation, Blackstaff Press, 1982

ROBERT GREACEN

b. 1920 in Derry. Brought up in Belfast, spent much of his life in London and now lives in Dublin. Educated at Methodist College Belfast, and Trinity College Dublin. Edited a number of anthologies, including *Poems from Ulster* (1942), *Northern Harvest: An Anthology of Ulster Writing* (1944) and, with Valentin Iremonger, *The Faber Book of Contemporary Irish Poetry* (1949). Moved to London in the late 1940s. His autobiography, *Even Without Irene*, was published by the Dolmen Press in 1969. His other publications include *The Art of Noël Coward* (1953) and *The World of C.P. Snow* (1962).

POETRY COLLECTIONS BY ROBERT GREACEN

One Recent Evening, Favil Press, 1944
The Undying Day, Falcon Press, 1948
A Garland for Captain Fox, Gallery Press, 1975
I, Brother Stephen, Profile Poetry, 1978

Young Mr Gibbon, Profile Poetry, 1979
A Bright Mask: New and Selected Poems, Dedalus Press, 1985
Carnival at the River, Dedalus Press, 1990

ABOUT ROBERT GREACEN

Brown , Terence. 'Robert Greacen and Roy McFadden: apocalypse
and survival', in *Northern Voices: Poets from Ulster*, Gill and
Macmillan, 1975, pp. 128–40

SEAMUS HEANEY

b. 1939 in County Derry. Educated at St Columb's College, Derry, and
Queen's University Belfast, where he was a lecturer in English from 1966
to 1972. Spent one year of that time as visiting lecturer at the University
of California at Berkeley. Moved to County Wicklow in 1972 and
worked for a time as a freelance journalist and broadcaster. Later moved
to Dublin, where he taught at Carysfort College. He has been Boylston
Professor of Rhetoric and Oratory at Harvard University and, since 1989,
Professor of Poetry at Oxford University. Has received numerous
awards and prizes, including the Somerset Maugham Award (1968), the
American Irish Foundation Award (1972), the Denis Devlin Award
(1973), the Duff Cooper Award (1975), the W.H. Smith Literary Award
(1976), and the Bennett Award (1982). He co-edited, with Ted Hughes,
the anthology *The Rattle Bag* (Faber and Faber, 1982). *Preoccupations:
Selected Prose 1968–1978* (1980) and *The Government of the Tongue* (1988)
were both published by Faber and Faber. *The Cure at Troy*, his version
of Sophocles' tragedy *Philoctetes* ,will be published by Field Day / Faber
and Faber in 1990.

POETRY COLLECTIONS BY SEAMUS HEANEY

Death of a Naturalist, Faber and Faber, 1966
Door into the Dark, Faber and Faber, 1969
Wintering Out, Faber and Faber, 1972
North, Faber and Faber, 1975
Field Work, Faber and Faber, 1979
Selected Poems 1965–1975, Faber and Faber, 1980
Sweeney Astray: A Version from the Irish, Field Day/Faber and Faber, 1983
Hailstones, Gallery Press, 1984
Station Island, Faber and Faber, 1984
The Haw Lantern, Faber and Faber, 1987
New Selected Poems 1966–1987, Faber and Faber, 1990

ABOUT SEAMUS HEANEY

Agenda, vol. 27, no. 1 (Spring 1989): special issue to mark Heaney's
  fiftieth birthday

Andrews, Elmer. *The Poetry of Seamus Heaney: All the Realms of
  Whisper*, Macmillan, 1988

Brown, Terence. 'Four new voices: poets of the present', in *Northern
  Voices: Poets from Ulster*, Gill and Macmillan, 1975, pp. 171–213

Buttel, Robert. *Seamus Heaney*, Bucknell University Press, 1975

Corcoran, Neil. *Seamus Heaney*, Faber and Faber, 1986

Curtis, Tony (ed.). *The Art of Seamus Heaney*, Poetry Wales Press,
  1982; revised edition, 1985

Deane, Seamus. 'Seamus Heaney: the timorous and the bold', in *Celtic
  Revivals: Essays in Modern Irish Literature 1880–1980*, Faber and
  Faber, 1985, pp. 174–88

Foster, John Wilson. 'Seamus Heaney's *A Lough Neagh Sequence:*
  sources and motifs', *Éire–Ireland* (Summer 1977), pp. 138–42

Foster, Tom. *Seamus Heaney*, O'Brien Press, 1989

Garratt, Robert F. 'The poetry of commitment: Seamus Heaney', in
  Modern Irish Poetry: Tradition and Continuity from Yeats to Heaney,
  University of California Press, 1986, pp. 230–58

Haffenden, John (ed.). *Viewpoints: Poets in Conversation*, Faber and
  Faber, 1981, pp. 57–75

Hederman, Mark Patrick. 'Seamus Heaney: the reluctant poet', *Crane
  Bag*, vol. 3, no. 2 (1979), pp. 61–70

Johnston, Dillon. 'Kavanagh and Heaney', in *Irish Poetry after Joyce*,
  University of Notre Dame Press, 1985, pp. 121–66

Kearney, Timothy. '"Befitting emblems of adversity": Seamus Heaney,
  the poet and the Troubles', *Threshold*, no. 32 (Winter 1982),
  pp. 67–77

Longley, Edna. ' "Inner emigré" or "Artful voyeur?": Seamus Heaney's
  North', in *Poetry in the Wars*, Bloodaxe Books, 1986, pp. 140–69

Longley, Edna. 'Putting on the international style', *Irish Review*, no. 5
  (Autumn 1988), pp. 75–81

Lysaght, Seán. 'Heaney *vs* Praeger: contrasting natures', *Irish Review*,
  no. 7 (Autumn 1989), pp. 68–74

McGuinness, Arthur E. ' "Hoarder of the common ground": tradition
  and ritual in Seamus Heaney's poetry', *Éire–Ireland* (Summer 1978),
  pp. 71–92

Morrison, Blake. *Seamus Heaney*, Methuen, 1982

Tamplin, Ronald. *Seamus Heaney*, Open University Press, 1989

RECORDINGS

The Northern Muse: Seamus Heaney and John Montague Reading their own Poems, Claddagh Records, Dublin, 1968
Seamus Heaney and Tom Paulin, Faber Poetry Cassettes, 1983

JOHN HEWITT

b. 1907 in Belfast, d. 1987. Educated at Methodist College Belfast, and Queen's University Belfast. On the staff of the Belfast Museum and Art Gallery, 1930–57. Art director of the Herbert Art Gallery and Museum, Coventry, 1957–72. Editor and art critic as well as poet. Wrote monographs on the Ulster painters Colin Middleton (1970) and John Luke (1978). Published *Art in Ulster 1* (1977). Associate editor of the magazine *Lagan*, and poetry editor of *Threshold* from 1957 to 1962. Edited *The Poems of William Allingham* (1967) and *Rhyming Weavers* (1974). Was the first writer-in-residence at Queen's University, 1976–9. Made a freeman of the city of Belfast in 1983 and awarded an honorary Ph.D. by Queen's University in the same year. Awarded the Gregory Medal by the Irish Academy of Letters in 1984. *Ancestral Voices: The Selected Prose of John Hewitt* (edited and with an introduction by Tom Clyde) was published by Blackstaff Press in 1987.

POETRY COLLECTIONS BY JOHN HEWITT

No Rebel Word, Frederick Muller, 1948
Collected Poems 1932–1967, MacGibbon and Kee, 1968
The Day of the Corncrake: Poems of the Nine Glens, Glens of Antrim
  Historical Society, 1969; revised edition, 1984
Out of My Time, Blackstaff Press, 1974
Time Enough, Blackstaff Press, 1976
The Rain Dance, Blackstaff Press, 1978
Kites in Spring: A Belfast Boyhood, Blackstaff Press, 1980
The Selected John Hewitt, edited and with an introduction by Alan
  Warner, Blackstaff Press, 1981
Mosaic, Blackstaff Press, 1982
Loose Ends, Blackstaff Press, 1983
Freehold and Other Poems, Blackstaff Press, 1986

ABOUT JOHN HEWITT

Brown, Terence. 'John Hewitt: land and people', in *Northern Voices: Poets from Ulster*, Gill and Macmillan, 1975, pp. 86–97
Fortnight, no. 275 (July/August 1989), contains a Hewitt supplement

Foster, John Wilson. 'The landscape of the Planter and the Gael in the poetry of John Hewitt and John Montague', *Canadian Journal of Irish Studies*, vol. 1, no. 2 (November 1975), pp. 17–33

Foster, John Wilson. ' "The dissidence of dissent": John Hewitt and W.R. Rodgers', in *Across a Roaring Hill: The Protestant Imagination in Modern Ireland*, edited by Gerald Dawe and Edna Longley, Blackstaff Press, 1985, pp. 139–60

Grennan, Eamon. Review article on Hewitt's *Out of My Time* and *Time Enough*, *Éire–Ireland* (Summer 1977), pp. 143–51

Heaney, Seamus. 'The poetry of John Hewitt', *Threshold*, no. 22 (Summer 1969), pp. 73–7; reprinted in Heaney's *Preoccupations: Selected Prose 1968–1978*, Faber and Faber, 1980, pp. 207–10

Kearney, Timothy (interviewer). '"Beyond the Planter and the Gael": an interview with John Hewitt and John Montague', *Crane Bag*, vol. 4, no. 2 (1980–1), pp. 85–92

Longley, Edna. 'Progressive bookmen: politics and northern Protestant writers since the 1930s', *Irish Review*, no. 1 (1986), pp. 50–7

Montague, John. 'Regionalism into reconciliation: the poetry of John Hewitt', *Poetry Ireland*, no. 13 (Spring 1964), pp. 113–18

Mooney, Martin. ' "A native mode": language and regionalism in the poetry of John Hewitt', *Irish Review*, no. 3 (1988), pp. 67–74

Mullan, Fiona. 'Paved unerring roads: the poetry of John Hewitt', *Threshold*, no. 36 (Winter 1985–6), pp. 30–43

Olinder, Britt. 'John Hewitt's Belfast', in *The Irish Writer and the City*, edited by Maurice Harmon, Colin Smythe, 1984, pp. 144–52

Sealy, Douglas. 'An individual flavour: the collected poems of John Hewitt', *Dublin Magazine*, vol. 8, nos 1–2 (Spring/Summer 1969), pp. 19–24

Threshold, no. 38 (Winter 1986–7), a special John Hewitt number

RECORDING

Shadow and Substance, cassette, Audio Arts, London, 1980

FILM

I Found Myself Alone, Arts Council of Northern Ireland, 1978

JOHN HUGHES

b. 1962 in Belfast. Educated at St Patrick's High School, Downpatrick, and Queen's University Belfast, where he took a degree in English. Currently lives and works in the USA.

POETRY COLLECTION BY JOHN HUGHES
The Something in Particular, Gallery Press, 1986

ROBERT JOHNSTONE

b. 1951 in Belfast. Educated at the Royal Belfast Academical Institution and the New University of Ulster. Co-founder and co-editor of the literary magazine *Caret,* with William Peskett and Trevor McMahon. From 1974 to 1986 he was associated with *Fortnight* magazine, as film critic, reviewer and deputy editor. Co-editor, with Frank Ormsby, of the *Honest Ulsterman*, which he now edits with Ruth Hooley. His publications include *Images of Belfast* (Blackstaff Press, 1983) and, as editor, *All Shy Wildness* (Blackstaff Press, 1984), an anthology of animal poems by Irish writers. He now lives in London.

POETRY COLLECTIONS BY ROBERT JOHNSTONE

Breakfast in a Bright Room, Blackstaff Press, 1983
Eden to Edenderry, Blackstaff Press, 1989

MICHAEL LONGLEY

b. 1939 in Belfast. Educated at the Royal Belfast Academical Institution, and Trinity College Dublin, where he read Classics. Won an Eric Gregory Award in 1965 and the award of the American Irish Foundation in 1985 . Edited *Over the Moon and Under the Stars* (Arts Council of Northern Ireland, 1971), an anthology of children's poetry from Northern Ireland, *Causeway: The Arts in Ulster* (Arts Council of Northern Ireland, 1971) and Louis MacNeice's *Selected Poems* (Faber and Faber, 1988). Now works as Combined Arts Director with the Arts Council of Northern Ireland.

POETRY COLLECTIONS BY MICHAEL LONGLEY

No Continuing City, Macmillan, 1969
An Exploded View, Gollancz, 1973
Man Lying on a Wall, Gollancz, 1976
The Echo Gate, Secker and Warburg, 1979
Selected Poems 1963–1980 ,Wake Forest University Press, 1981
Poems 1963–1983, Salamander Press, 1984; Penguin Books, 1985
Gorse Fires, Secker and Warburg, forthcoming, 1991

ABOUT MICHAEL LONGLEY

Allen, Michael. 'Options: the poetry of Michael Longley', *Éire–Ireland* (Winter 1975), pp. 129–36

Brown, Terence. 'Four new voices: poets of the present', in *Northern Voices: Poets from Ulster,* Gill and Macmillan, 1975, pp. 171–213

Dawe, Gerald. '"Icon and Lares": Derek Mahon and Michael Longley', in *Across a Roaring Hill: The Protestant Imagination in Modern Ireland,* edited by Gerald Dawe and Edna Longley, Blackstaff Press, 1985, pp. 218–35

Johnstone, Robert (interviewer). 'The Longley tapes', *Honest Ulsterman,* no. 78 (Summer 1985), pp. 13–31

RECORDING

Words Alone: Michael Longley and Derek Mahon Reading their own Poems, Outlet Recordings, Belfast, 1968

PETER MCDONALD

b. 1962 in Belfast. Educated at Methodist College Belfast, and University College, Oxford. He has been a junior research fellow of Christ Church, Oxford, and is now a fellow and lecturer in English at Pembroke College, Cambridge. Selections of his poems appeared in the anthologies *Trio Poetry 3* (Blackstaff Press, 1982), *New Chatto Poets* (Chatto and Windus, 1986) and *Map-Makers' Colours: New Poets of Northern Ireland* (Nu-Age Editions, Montreal, 1988). In 1983 he won the Newdigate Prize for Poetry, and in 1987 an Eric Gregory Award. His critical study *Louis MacNeice: The Poet in his Contexts* was published by Oxford University Press in 1990.

POETRY COLLECTION BY PETER MCDONALD

Biting the Wax, Bloodaxe Books, 1989

ROY MCFADDEN

b. 1921 in Belfast. Educated at Methodist College Belfast, and Queen's University Belfast. Practised law in Belfast until his retirement. Emerged as a poet in the 1940s, joint-edited the magazine *Rann* with Barbara Hunter from 1948 to 1953, edited *Ulster Voices* (1943) and *Irish Voices* (1943), with Robert Greacen, and was an associate editor of *Lagan*. First appeared in book form, with Alex Comfort and Ian Serraillier, in the anthology *Three*

New Poets (Grey Walls Press, 1942). Among his other poetry publications were *Russian Summer* (Gayfield, 1941) and *Elegy for the Dead of the Princess Victoria* (Lisnagarvey Press, 1943).

POETRY COLLECTIONS BY ROY MCFADDEN

Swords and Ploughshares, Routledge, 1943
Flowers for a Lady, Routledge, 1945
The Heart's Townland, Routledge, 1947
The Garryowen, Chatto and Windus, 1971
Verifications, Blackstaff Press, 1977
A Watching Brief, Blackstaff Press, 1979
The Selected Roy McFadden, Blackstaff Press, 1983
Letters to the Hinterland, Dedalus Press, 1986
After Seymour's Funeral, Blackstaff Press, 1990

ABOUT ROY MCFADDEN

Brown, Terence. 'Robert Greacen and Roy McFadden: apocalypse and survival', in *Northern Voices: Poets from Ulster*, Gill and Macmillan, 1975, pp. 128–40
Boyd, John. Introduction to *The Selected Roy McFadden*, Blackstaff Press, 1983

MEDBH MCGUCKIAN

b. 1950 in Belfast. Educated at the Dominican College, Fortwilliam, Belfast, and at Queen's University Belfast, where she took a BA in English and an MA in Anglo-Irish literature. Won the Poetry Society Competition in 1979 and an Eric Gregory Award in 1980. Published two pamphlet collections of poems: *Portrait of Joanna* (Ulsterman Publications, 1980) and *Single Ladies* (Interim Press, 1980) and was represented in the anthologies *Trio Poetry 2* (Blackstaff Press, 1981) and *Introductions 5* (Faber and Faber, 1982). Her first book collection, *The Flower Master* (1982), won the Rooney Prize and the Alice Hunt Bartlett Award. Writer-in-residence at Queen's University Belfast from 1985 to 1988. Literary editor of *Fortnight* magazine since 1989. Edited *The Big Striped Golfing Umbrella* (Arts Council of Northern Ireland, 1985), an anthology of children's poetry from Northern Ireland.

POETRY COLLECTIONS BY MEDBH MCGUCKIAN

The Flower Master, Oxford University Press, 1982

Venus and the Rain, Oxford University Press, 1984
On Ballycastle Beach, Oxford University Press, 1988
Two Women, Two Shores (with Nuala Archer), New Poets Series,
   Baltimore, Maryland, 1989

ABOUT MEDBH MCGUCKIAN

Wills, Clair. 'The perfect mother: authority in the poetry of Medbh
   McGuckian', *Text and Context,* no. 3 (Autumn 1988), pp. 91–111

LOUIS MACNEICE

b. 1907 in Belfast, d. 1963. Father became rector of St Nicholas's Church,
Carrickfergus, in 1908. Mother died of tuberculosis in 1914. Attended
Sherbourne Preparatory School in Dorset, 1917–21, and Marlborough
College, Wiltshire, 1921–6. Read Classics and Philosophy at Oxford,
1926–30. Appointed lecturer in Classics at Birmingham University,
1930. Joined BBC as scriptwriter and producer in 1941. Broadcast a
number of plays and wrote many other scripts for radio. In addition to
poetry and translations, he published *Modern Poetry: A Personal Essay*
(1938). *The Strings Are False,* an unfinished autobiography, appeared in
1965. *Selected Literary Criticism of Louis MacNeice* (1987), and *Selected Prose
of Louis MacNeice* (1990), both edited by Alan Heuser, are published by
Oxford University Press.

POETRY COLLECTIONS BY LOUIS MACNEICE

Collected Poems, Faber and Faber, 1966; new edition, 1969, paperback,
   1979
Selected Poems, edited by W.H. Auden, Faber and Faber, 1964
Selected Poems, edited by Michael Longley, Faber and Faber, 1988

ABOUT LOUIS MACNEICE

Brown, Terence. *Louis MacNeice: Sceptical Vision,* Gill and
   Macmillan, 1975
Brown, Terence and Alec Reid (eds). *Time Was Away: The World of
   Louis MacNeice,* Dolmen Press, 1974
Coulton, Barbara. *Louis MacNeice in the BBC,* Faber and Faber, 1980
Honest Ulsterman, no. 73 (September 1983), a special MacNeice
   number
Longley, Edna. *Louis MacNeice,* Faber and Faber, 1988
McDonald, Peter. *Louis MacNeice: The Poet in his Contexts,* Oxford
   University Press, 1990

McKinnon, William T. *Apollo's Blended Dream*, Oxford University
Press, 1971
Marsack, Robyn. *The Cave of Making: The Poetry of Louis MacNeice*,
Oxford University Press, 1982
Moore, D.B. *The Poetry of Louis MacNeice*, Leicester University Press,
1972
Smith, Elton Edward. *Louis MacNeice*, Twayne Publishers Inc., 1970

RECORDING

Louis MacNeice Reads Selected Poems, Argo, London, 1961

DEREK MAHON

b. 1941 in Belfast. Educated at the Royal Belfast Academical Institution
and Trinity College Dublin. Won an Eric Gregory Award in 1965. Has
worked as a teacher in Ireland, Canada and the USA, and as a journalist
in London, where he was features editor of *Vogue* and literary editor of
the *New Statesman*. Was poet-in-residence at the New University of
Ulster and at Trinity College Dublin. Edited *The Sphere Book of Modern
Irish Poetry* (1972). His work as a translator from the French includes:
a version of Gérard de Nerval's *The Chimeras* (Gallery Press, 1982); *High
Time* (Gallery Press, 1985), a version of Molière's *The School for Hus-
bands;* a version of Molière's *The School for Wives* (Gallery Press, 1986);
and the *Selected Poems* of Philippe Jaccottet (Penguin, 1988). Co-editor,
with Peter Fallon, of *The Penguin Book of Contemporary Irish Poetry* (1990).

POETRY COLLECTIONS BY DEREK MAHON

Night-Crossing. Oxford University Press, 1968
Lives, Oxford University Press, 1972
The Snow Party, Oxford University Press, 1975
Poems 1962–1978, Oxford University Press, 1979
Courtyards in Delft, Gallery Press, 1981
The Hunt by Night, Oxford University Press, 1982
Antarctica, Gallery Press, 1985
Selected Poems, Penguin, forthcoming, 1991

ABOUT DEREK MAHON

Brown, Terence. 'Four new voices: poets of the present', in *Northern
Voices: Poets from Ulster*, Gill and Macmillan, 1975, pp. 171–213
Byrne, John. 'Derek Mahon: a commitment to change', *Crane Bag*,
vol. 6, no. 1 (1982), pp. 62–72

Dawe, Gerald. '"Icon and Lares": Derek Mahon and Michael
   Longley, in *Across a Roaring Hill: The Protestant Imagination in
   Modern Ireland*, edited by Gerald Dawe and Edna Longley,
   Blackstaff Press, 1985, pp. 218–35
Deane, Seamus. 'Derek Mahon: freedom from history', in *Celtic
   Revivals: Essays in Modern Irish Literature 1880–1980*, Faber and
   Faber, 1985, pp. 156–65
Dunn, Douglas. 'Let the God not abandon us: on the poetry of Derek
   Mahon', *Stone Ferry Review*, no. 2 (Winter 1978), pp. 7–30
Frazer, Adrian. 'Proper portion: Derek Mahon's *The Hunt by Night*',
   Éire–Ireland, vol. 18, no. 4 (Winter 1983), pp. 136–43
Johnston, Dillon. 'MacNeice and Mahon', in *Irish Poetry after Joyce*,
   University of Notre Dame Press, 1985, pp. 204–46
Kelly, Willie (interviewer). ' "Each poem for me is a new beginning":
   interview with Derek Mahon', *Cork Review*, vol. 2, no. 3 (June
   1981), pp. 10–12
Kennelly, Brendan. 'Derek Mahon's humane perspective', in *Tradition
   and Influence in Anglo-Irish Poetry*, edited by Terence Brown and
   Nicholas Grene, Macmillan, 1989, pp. 143–52
Longley, Edna. 'The singing line: form in Derek Mahon's poetry', in
   Poetry in the Wars, Bloodaxe Books, 1986, pp. 170–84
Mullaney, Kathleen. 'A poetics of silence: Derek Mahon "At One
   Remove" ', *Journal of Irish Literature*, vol. 18, no. 3 (September
   1989), pp. 45–54
Patton, Eve (interviewer). 'Translations: an interview with Derek
   Mahon', *Rhinoceros*, no. 3, pp. 81–90

RECORDINGS

*Words Alone: Michael Longley and Derek Mahon Reading their own
   Poems*, Outlet Recordings, Belfast, 1968
Derek Mahon Reads his own Poetry, Claddagh Records, Dublin, 1973

TOM MATTHEWS

b. 1945 in Ballymena, County Antrim, and brought up in Derry. Educated at Foyle College, Derry, and Queen's University Belfast. Worked for a time in Larne, County Antrim, as a chemist in a cement works. His pamphlet collections *Interior Din* (1968) and *Foolstop* (1973) were both issued by Ulsterman Publications. He now lives and works in London.

POETRY COLLECTION BY TOM MATTHEWS

Dr Wilson as an Arab, Holysmoke Press, 1974

JOHN MONTAGUE

b. 1929 in Brooklyn, New York. Moved to County Tyrone in1933 to live on his aunts' farm. Educated at St Patrick's College, Armagh, and University College Dublin. Studied and taught in the USA, 1953–6. Lived in Dublin and Paris. Lecturer at University College Cork from 1972 to 1988. Editor of *The Faber Book of Irish Verse* (1974), and *Bitter Harvest* (Scribner's, 1989), an anthology of contemporary Irish poetry. He also published a collection of short stories, *Death of a Chieftain* (MacGibbon and Kee, 1964; Poolbeg Press, 1978), an autobiographical prose work, *The Lost Notebook* (Mercier Press, 1987), and a collection of essays, *The Figure in the Cave and Other Essays*, edited by Antoinette Quinn (Lilliput Press, 1989).

POETRY COLLECTIONS BY JOHN MONTAGUE

Poisoned Lands, MacGibbon and Kee, 1961; revised edition, Dolmen
  Press, 1977
A Chosen Light, MacGibbon and Kee, 1967
Tides, Dolmen Press, 1970
The Rough Field, Dolmen Press/Blackstaff Press, 1972
A Slow Dance, Dolmen Press, 1975
The Great Cloak, Dolmen Press, 1978
Selected Poems, Dolmen Press, 1982
The Dead Kingdom, Dolmen Press/Blackstaff Press, 1984
Mount Eagle, Gallery Press, 1988
New Selected Poems, Gallery Press, 1989

ABOUT JOHN MONTAGUE

Brown, Terence. 'John Montague: circling to return', in *Northern
  Voices: Poets from Ulster*, Gill and Macmillan, 1975, pp. 149–70
Deane, Seamus. 'John Montague: the kingdom of the dead', in *Celtic
  Revivals: Essays in Modern Irish Literature 1880–1980*, Faber and
  Faber, 1985, pp. 146–55
Foster, John Wilson. 'The landscape of the Planter and the Gael in
  the poetry of John Hewitt and John Montague', *Canadian Journal
  of Irish Studies*, vol. 1, no. 2 (November 1975), pp. 17–33
Frazer, Adrian. 'Interview with John Montague', *Literary Review*,
  vol. 22, no. 2 (Winter 1979), pp. 153–4

Garratt, Robert F. 'Poetry at mid-century I: John Montague', in
    Modern Irish Poetry: Tradition and Continuity from Yeats to Heaney,
    University of California Press, 1986, pp. 198–229
Irish University Review, vol. 19, no. 1 (Spring 1989), edited by
    Christopher Murray; a special John Montague issue
Johnston, Dillon. 'Devlin and Montague', in *Irish Poetry after Joyce*,
    University of Notre Dame Press, 1985, pp. 167–203
Kearney, Timothy (interviewer). '"Beyond the Planter and the Gael":
    an interview with John Hewitt and John Montague', *Crane Bag*,
    vol. 4, no. 2 (1980–1), pp. 85–92
Kersnowski, Frank. *John Montague*, Bucknell University Press, 1975
Longley, Edna. 'Searching the darkness: Richard Murphy,
    Thomas Kinsella, John Montague and James Simmons', in *Two
    Decades of Irish Writing: A Critical Survey*, edited by Douglas
    Dunn, Carcanet Press, 1975, pp. 118–53
Lucy, Sean. 'Three poets from Ulster', *Irish University Review*, vol. 3,
    no. 2 (Autumn 1973), pp. 179–93
Maxwell, D.E.S. 'The poetry of John Montague', *Critical Quarterly*,
    vol. 15, no. 2 (Summer 1973), pp. 180–5
Redshaw, Thomas Dillon. 'John Montague's *The Rough Field*: Topos
    and Texne', *Studies*, vol. 61 (Spring 1974), pp. 31–46
Redshaw, Thomas Dillon (ed.). *Hill Field: Poems and Memoirs for John
    Montague on his Sixtieth Birthday*, Coffee House Press,
    Minneapolis/Gallery Press, 1989
Weatherhead, A.K. 'John Montague: exiled from order', *Concerning
    Poetry*, vol. 14, no. 2 (Fall 1981), pp. 97–101

RECORDING

*The Northern Muse: Seamus Heaney and John Montague Reading their
    own Poems*, Claddagh Records, Dublin, 1968

PAUL MULDOON

b. 1951 in County Armagh and grew up near the Moy, County Tyrone.
Educated at St Patrick's College, Armagh, and Queen's University
Belfast. Won an Eric Gregory Award in 1972. Has worked as a producer
for the BBC and taught at Cambridge, Columbia and Princeton. He
edited *The Scrake of Dawn* (Blackstaff Press/Arts Council of Northern

Ireland, 1979), an anthology of poems by young people from Northern Ireland, and, in 1986, *The Faber Book of Contemporary Irish Poetry*. Now lives and works in the USA.

POETRY COLLECTIONS BY PAUL MULDOON

New Weather, Faber and Faber, 1973
Mules, Faber and Faber, 1977
Why Brownlee Left, Faber and Faber, 1980
Quoof, Faber and Faber, 1983
The Wishbone, Gallery Press, 1984
Selected Poems 1968–1983, Faber and Faber, 1986
Meeting the British, Faber and Faber, 1987
Madoc: A Mystery, Faber and Faber, 1990

ABOUT PAUL MULDOON

Frazer, Adrian. 'Juniper, otherwise known: poems by Paulin and Muldoon', *Éire–Ireland*, vol. 19, no. 1 (Spring 1984), pp. 123–33
Haffenden, John (ed.). *Viewpoints: Poets in Conversation*, Faber and Faber, 1981, pp. 130–42
Heaney, Seamus. *Preoccupations: Selected Prose 1968–1978*, Faber and Faber, 1980, pp. 211–13
Johnston, Dillon. 'Toward "a broader and more comprehensive Irish identity" ', in *Irish Poetry after Joyce*, University of Notre Dame Press, 1985, pp. 247–72
Longley, Edna. 'Varieties of parable: Louis MacNeice and Paul Muldoon', *Poetry in the Wars*, Bloodaxe Books, 1986, pp. 211–43

RECORDING

Ted Hughes and Paul Muldoon, Faber Poetry Cassettes, 1983

FRANK ORMSBY

b. 1947 in Enniskillen, County Fermanagh. Educated at St Michael's College, Enniskillen, and Queen's University Belfast. Has taught English at the Royal Belfast Academical Institution since 1971. Edited the *Honest Ulsterman*, jointly or alone, from 1969 to 1989. Has also edited *Northern Windows: An Anthology of Ulster Autobiography* (1987), *The Long Embrace: Twentieth-century Irish Love Poems* (1987) and *Thine in Storm and Calm: An Amanda McKittrick Ros Reader* (1988), all published by Blackstaff Press.

315

POETRY COLLECTIONS BY FRANK ORMSBY

A Store of Candles, Oxford University Press, 1977; re-issued by Gallery
    Press, 1986
A Northern Spring, Secker and Warburg/Gallery Press, 1986

TOM PAULIN

b. 1949 in Leeds. Grew up in Belfast, where he attended Annadale
Grammar School. Educated also at the University of Hull and at Oxford.
Won an Eric Gregory Award in 1976 and a Somerset Maugham Award
in 1978. Lectures in English at the University of Nottingham and has
been a visiting lecturer at the University of Virginia. A founder-member
and director of the Field Day Theatre Company. In addition to his
collections of poems, he has published: a critical work, *Thomas Hardy:
The Poetry of Perception* (Macmillan, 1975); a play, *The Riot Act* (Faber
and Faber, 1985), which is a version of Sophocles' *Antigone; Ireland and
the English Crisis* (Bloodaxe Books, 1985), a collection of essays and
reviews; *The Hillsborough Script: A Dramatic Satire* (Faber and Faber,
1987); and *Seize the Fire* (Faber and Faber, 1990), a version of Aeschylus'
Prometheus Bound. He also edited *The Faber Book of Political Verse* (1986).

POETRY COLLECTIONS BY TOM PAULIN

A State of Justice, Faber and Faber, 1977
The Strange Museum, Faber and Faber, 1980; reissued 1987
Liberty Tree, Faber and Faber, 1983
Fivemiletown, Faber and Faber, 1987

ABOUT TOM PAULIN

Frazer, Adrian. 'Juniper, otherwise known: poems by Paulin and
    Muldoon', *Éire–Ireland*, vol. 19, no. 1 (Spring 1984), pp. 123–33
Haffenden, John (ed.). *Viewpoints: Poets in Conversation*, Faber and
    Faber, 1981, pp. 157–73

RECORDING

Seamus Heaney and Tom Paulin, Faber Poetry Cassettes, 1983

WILLIAM PESKETT

b. 1952 in Cambridge. Came to live in Belfast in 1959. Educated at the
Royal Belfast Academical Institution, and Christ's College, Cambridge,

where he read zoology. Co-edited the literary magazine *Caret*. Won an Eric Gregory Award in 1976. Worked in Suffolk as a teacher of biology, then as a journalist in London, where he now lives.

POETRY COLLECTIONS BY WILLIAM PESKETT

The Night-owl's Dissection, Secker and Warburg, 1975
Survivors, Secker and Warburg, 1980

W.R. RODGERS

b. 1909 in Belfast, d. 1969 in Los Angeles. Graduated from Queen's University Belfast in 1931. Ordained in 1935 and appointed Presbyterian minister at Loughgall, County Armagh. Joined BBC in London in 1946. Lived at various times in Suffolk, Essex and California. Buried in Loughgall.

POETRY COLLECTIONS BY W.R. RODGERS

Awake! and Other Poems, Secker and Warburg, 1941
Europa and the Bull, Secker and Warburg, 1952
Collected Poems, Oxford University Press, 1971

ABOUT W.R RODGERS

Amis, Kingsley. 'Ulster bull: the case of W.R. Rodgers', *Essays in Criticism*, vol. 3, no. 4 (October 1953), pp. 470–5
Brown, Terence. 'W.R. Rodgers: Romantic Calvinist', in *Northern Voices: Poets from Ulster*, Gill and Macmillan, 1975, pp. 114–27
Foster, John Wilson. ' "The dissidence of dissent": John Hewitt and W.R. Rodgers', in *Across a Roaring Hill: The Protestant Imagination in Modern Ireland*, edited by Gerald Dawe and Edna Longley, Blackstaff Press, 1985, pp. 139–60
O'Brien, Darcy. *W.R. Rodgers*, Bucknell University Press, 1970

RECORDING

Europa and the Bull: W.R. Rodgers Reading from his Second Volume, Argo, London, 1953–4

JAMES SIMMONS

b. 1933 in Derry. Educated at Foyle College, Derry, Campbell College, Belfast, and Leeds University, where he graduated in 1958. Taught at

Friends School, Lisburn, for five years and, for three years, at Ahmadu Bello University, Zaria, Nigeria. Returned from Africa in 1967 to lecture in drama and Anglo-Irish literature at the New University of Ulster. Founded the *Honest Ulsterman* magazine in 1968 and edited the first nineteen issues. Songwriter and singer as well as poet. Three LPs of his songs have been issued: *City and Eastern*, *Love in the Post* and *The Rostrevor Sessions*. Edited the anthology *Ten Irish Poets* (Carcanet Press, 1974) and has written a critical study, *Sean O'Casey* (Macmillan, 1983). Became writer-in-residence at Queen's University Belfast in 1988.

POETRY COLLECTIONS BY JAMES SIMMONS

Late but in Earnest, Bodley Head, 1967
In the Wilderness and Other Poems, Bodley Head, 1969
Energy to Burn, Bodley Head, 1971
No Land is Waste, Dr Eliot, Keepsake Press, 1972
The Long Summer Still to Come, Blackstaff Press, 1973
West Strand Visions, Blackstaff Press, 1974
Judy Garland and the Cold War, Blackstaff Press, 1976
The Selected James Simmons, edited and with an introduction by
    Edna Longley, Blackstaff Press, 1978
Constantly Singing, Blackstaff Press, 1980
From the Irish, Blackstaff Press, 1985
Poems 1956–1986, with an introduction by Edna Longley, Gallery
    Press/Bloodaxe Books, 1986

ABOUT JAMES SIMMONS

Brown, Terence. 'Four new voices: poets of the present', in *Northern Voices: Poets from Ulster*, Gill and Macmillan, 1975, pp. 171–213
Brown, Terence. 'Poets and patrimony: Richard Murphy and James Simmons', in *Across a Roaring Hill: The Protestant Imagination in Modern Ireland*, edited by Gerald Dawe and Edna Longley, Blackstaff Press, 1985, pp. 182–95
Longley, Edna. Introductions to *The Selected James Simmons*, (Blackstaff Press, 1978) and *Poems 1956–1986* (Gallery Press/ Bloodaxe Books, 1986)
Mooney, Martin (interviewer). 'Still burning: James Simmons in conversation with Martin Mooney', *Rhinoceros*, no. 2, pp. 101–22

PATRICK WILLIAMS

b. 1950 in County Down. Educated at Trinity College Dublin. Has worked in London and Canada. Now lives in Belfast where he was, for a time, poetry editor of the *Belfast Review*.

POETRY COLLECTION BY PATRICK WILLIAMS

Trails, Sidgwick and Jackson,1981

SELECT BIBLIOGRAPHY

GENERAL

Andrews, Elmer (ed.). *Contemporary Irish Poetry: A Collection of Critical Essays*, Macmillan, 1990

Bell, Sam Hanna. *The Theatre in Ulster*, Gill and Macmillan, 1972

Bell, Sam Hanna, Nesca A. Robb and John Hewitt (eds). *The Arts In Ulster*, Harrap, 1951

Brown, Terence. *Northern Voices: Poets from Ulster*, Gill and Macmillan, 1975

Brown, Terence. *Ireland's Literature: Selected Essays*, Lilliput Press, 1988

Brown, Terence and Nicholas Grene (eds). *Tradition and Influence in Anglo-Irish Poetry*, Macmillan, 1989

Carney, James. *The Irish Bardic Poet*, Dolmen Press, 1967

Catto, Mike. *Art in Ulster 2*, Blackstaff Press, 1977

Corcoran, Neil (ed.). *The Chosen Ground: Essays on the Contemporary Poetry of Northern Ireland*, Poetry Wales Press/Severn Books, forthcoming, 1991

Dawe, Gerald and Edna Longley (eds). *Across a Roaring Hill: The Protestant Imagination in Modern Ireland*, Blackstaff Press, 1985

Deane, Seamus. *Celtic Revivals: Essays in Modern Irish Literature 1880–1980*, Faber and Faber, 1985

Deane, Seamus. *A Short History of Irish Literature*, Hutchinson, 1986

Doloughan, Phyllis E. 'Ulster poetry: a checklist of published collections 1960–1980', Department of Library and Information Studies, Queen's University Belfast, 1983

Donoghue, Denis. *We Irish: Selected Essays of Denis Donoghue*, vol. 1, Harvester, 1986

Dunn, Douglas (ed.). *Two Decades of Irish Writing: A Critical Survey*, Carcanet Press, 1975

Foster, John Wilson. *Forces and Themes in Ulster Fiction*, Gill and Macmillan, 1974

Garratt, Robert F. *Modern Irish Poetry: Tradition and Continuity from Yeats to Heaney*, University of California Press, 1986

Haffenden, John (ed.). *Viewpoints: Poets in Conversation*, Faber and Faber, 1981

Harmon, Maurice (ed.). *The Irish Writer and the City*, Colin Smythe, 1984

Hewitt, John. *Art in Ulster 1*, Blackstaff Press, 1977

Johnston, Dillon. *Irish Poetry after Joyce*, University of Notre Dame Press, 1985

Kennelly, Michael (ed.). *Cultural Contexts and Literary Idioms*, Colin
Smythe, 1989
Longley, Edna. *Poetry in the Wars*, Bloodaxe Books, 1986
Longley, Michael. *Causeway: The Arts in Ulster*, Arts Council of
Northern Ireland, 1971

ARTICLES

Buckley, Vincent. 'Poetry and the avoidance of nationalism',
Threshold, no. 32 (Winter 1982), pp. 8–34
Clyde, Tom. 'An Ulster Twilight? Poetry in the north of Ireland',
Krino, no. 5 (Spring 1988), pp. 95–102
Deane, Seamus. 'The writer and the Troubles', *Threshold*, no. 25
(Summer 1974), pp. 13–17
Dunn, Douglas. 'The speckled hill, the plover's shore: Northern Irish
poetry today', *Encounter*, vol. 61, no. 6 (December 1963),
pp. 70–6
Foster, John Wilson. 'Culture and colonisation: view from the north',
Irish Review, no. 5 (Autumn 1988), pp. 17–26
Fullwood, Daphne and Oliver Edwards. 'Ulster poetry since
1900', *Rann*, no. 20 (June 1953), pp. 19–34
Greacen, Robert. 'A survey of Ulster writing', *Northman*, vol. 11,
no. 2 (Winter 1942–3), pp. 10–14
Greacen, Robert. 'The Belfast poetry scene 1939–1945', *Honest
Ulsterman*, no. 77 (Winter 1984), pp. 17–22
Group, The. 'The Belfast group: a symposium', *Honest Ulsterman*,
no. 53 (November/December 1976), pp. 53–63
Hederman, Mark Patrick. 'Poetry and the Fifth Province', *Crane
Bag*, vol. 9, no. 1 (1985), pp. 110–19; *see also* Edna Longley's
reply in the same issue, pp. 120–2
Hewitt, John. ' "The bitter gourd": some problems of the Ulster
writer', *Lagan*, no. 3 (1945), pp. 93–105; reprinted in
Ancestral Voices: The Selected Prose of John Hewitt, edited by
Tom Clyde, Blackstaff Press, 1987, pp. 108–21
Hewitt, John. 'Poetry of Ulster: a survey', *Poetry Ireland*, no. 8
(January 1950), pp. 3–10
Hewitt, John. 'The course of writing in Ulster', *Rann*, no. 20 (June
1953), pp. 43–52; reprinted in *Ancestral Voices*, pp. 64–76
Kearney, Timothy. 'The poetry of the north: a post-modernist
perspective', *Crane Bag*, vol. 3, no. 2 (1979), pp. 45–53
Liddy, James. 'Ulster poets and the Catholic muse', *Éire–Ireland*
(Winter 1978), pp. 126–37

321

Longley, Edna. 'Stars and horses, pigs and trees', *Crane Bag*, vol. 3, no. 2 (1979), pp. 54–60

Longley, Edna. 'The writer and Belfast', in *The Irish Writer and the City*, edited by Maurice Harmon, Colin Smythe, 1984, pp. 65–89

Longley, Michael. 'Tu'penny Stung', in *Northern Windows: An Anthology of Ulster Autobiography*, edited by Frank Ormsby, Blackstaff Press, 1987, pp. 195–206

McFadden, Roy. 'The Belfast Forties', *Gown Literary Supplement* (June 1989), pp. 5–8

Mahon, Derek. 'Poetry in Northern Ireland', *Twentieth Century Studies*, no. 4 (November 1970), pp. 89–93

Mathews, Aidan Carl. 'A question of covenants: modern Irish poetry', *Crane Bag*, vol. 3, no. 1 (1979), pp. 48–57; *see also* Gerald Dawe's response in *Crane Bag*, vol. 3, no. 2 (1979), pp. 88–91

Quinn , Damian. 'The troubled poetry: recent poetry from Northern Ireland', *Prospice*, no. 20 (1987), pp. 69–81

Redshaw, Thomas Dillon. 'Rí, as in regional: three Ulster poets', *Éire–Ireland* (Summer 1974), pp. 41–64 (on Heaney, Deane and Montague)

Riordan, Maurice. 'Eros and history: on contemporary Irish poetry', *Crane Bag*, vol. 9, no. 1 (1985), pp. 49–55

Sergeant, Howard. 'Ulster regionalism', *Rann*, no. 20 (June 1953), pp. 3–7

Tracy, Robert. 'An Ireland/the poets have imagined', *Crane Bag*, vol. 3, no. 2 (1979), pp. 82–8

Waterman, Andrew. 'Ulsterectomy', in *Best of the Poetry Year 6*, compiled by Dannie Abse, Robson Books, 1979, pp. 42–57

ANTHOLOGIES

Bradley, Anthony. *Contemporary Irish Poetry*, University of California Press, 1980; new and revised edition, 1988

Dawe, Gerald. *The Younger Irish Poets*, Blackstaff Press, 1982; revised edition, forthcoming, 1991

Deane, Seamus (general editor) and Andrew Carpenter (associate editor).*The Field Day Anthology of Irish Writing c. 550–1990*, 3 vols, Field Day, forthcoming, 1991

Fallon, Peter and Derek Mahon. *The Penguin Book of Contemporary Irish Poetry*, Penguin Books, 1990

Fiacc, Padraic. *The Wearing of the Black: An Anthology of Contemporary Ulster Poetry*, Blackstaff Press, 1974

Greacen, Robert. *Poems from Ulster*, Erskine Mayne, 1942

Greacen, Robert. *Northern Harvest*, Derrick MacCord, 1944

Harmon, Maurice. *Irish Poetry after Yeats: Seven Poets*, Wolfhound Press, 1979

Hewitt, John. *Rhyming Weavers, and Other Country Poets of Antrim and Down*, Blackstaff Press, 1974

Hooley, Ruth. *The Female Line: Northern Irish Women Writers*, Northern Ireland Women's Rights Movement, 1985

Kennelly, Brendan. *The Penguin Book of Irish Verse*, Penguin Books, 1970; second edition, 1981

Kinsella, Thomas. *The New Oxford Book of Irish Verse*, Oxford University Press, 1986

Longley, Michael. *Over the Moon and Under the Stars: An Anthology of Children's Poetry from Ulster*, Arts Council of Northern Ireland, 1971

McGuckian, Medbh. *The Big Striped Golfing Umbrella: An Anthology of Children's Poetry from Northern Ireland*, Arts Council of Northern Ireland, 1985

Montague, John. *The Faber Book of Irish Verse*, Faber and Faber, 1974

Montague, John. *Bitter Harvest: An Anthology of Contemporary Irish Verse*, Scribner's, 1989

Morrison, Blake and Andrew Motion. *The Penguin Book of Contemporary British Poetry*, Penguin Books, 1982

Muldoon, Paul. *The Scrake of Dawn: Poems by Young People from Northern Ireland*, Blackstaff Press/Arts Council of Northern Ireland, 1979

Muldoon, Paul. *The Faber Book of Contemporary Irish Poetry*, Faber and Faber, 1986

Ormsby, Frank. *Northern Windows: An Anthology of Ulster Autobiography*, Blackstaff Press, 1987

Simmons, James. *Ten Irish Poets*, Carcanet Press, 1974

Swift, Todd and Martin Mooney. *Map-makers' Colours: New Poets of Northern Ireland*, Nu-age Editions, 1988

Trio Poetry 1. Will Colhoun, Robert Johnstone, David Park, Blackstaff Press, 1980

Trio Poetry 2. Damian Gorman, Medbh McGuckian, Douglas Marshall, Blackstaff Press, 1981

Trio Poetry 3. Johnston Kirkpatrick, Peter McDonald, Trevor McMahon, Blackstaff Press, 1982

Trio Poetry 4. Andrew Elliott, Leon McAuley, Ciaran O'Driscoll, Blackstaff Press, 1985

Trio Poetry 5. Dennis Greig, Martin Mooney, Janet Shepperson, Blackstaff Press, 1987

Trio Poetry 6. Angela Greene, Oliver Marshall, Patrick Ramsey, Blackstaff Press, 1990

ACKNOWLEDGEMENTS

Grateful acknowledgement is made to:

Bloodaxe Books for permission to reprint the following poems by Peter McDonald: 'Pleasures of the imagination', 'Christmas', 'Cash positive', 'Totalled' and 'Sunday in Great Tew' from *Biting the Wax* (1989)

Sandra Buchanan for permission to reprint the following poems by George Buchanan: 'War-and-peace' and 'Theatrical Venus' from *Bodily Responses* (Gaberbocchus Press, 1958); 'Conversation with strangers' from *Conversation with Strangers* (Gaberbocchus Press, 1961); 'Lyle Donaghy, poet, 1902–1949', and 'Revolutionary revolution' from *Minute-Book of a City* (Carcanet Press, 1972); 'I suddenly . . .', 'Song for straphangers', 'A speaker in the square' and 'Lewis Mumford' from *Inside Traffic* (Carcanet Press, 1976); and 'Jill's death' from *Possible Being* (Carcanet Press, 1980)

Lucy Rodgers Cohen for permission to reprint the following poems by W.R. Rodgers: 'Words', 'The lovers', 'The party' and 'Field day' from *Collected Poems* (Oxford University Press, 1971), © W.R. Rodgers 1941

Gerald Dawe for permission to reprint the following poems: 'Names' and 'Sheltering places' from *Sheltering Places* (Blackstaff Press, 1978)

Seamus Deane for permission to reprint the following poem: 'A schooling' from *Rumours* (Dolmen Press, 1977)

Dedalus Press for permission to reprint the following poems by Robert Greacen: 'The bird', 'Father and son', 'A summer day' and 'Captain Fox' from *A Bright Mask: New and Selected Poems* (1985); 'St Andrew's Day' and 'Carnival by the river' from *Carnival by the River* (1990)

Andrew Elliott for permission to reprint the following poems: 'The stay behind', 'The love poem', 'The X-ray', 'Angel' and 'Here today . . .' from *The Creationists* (Blackstaff Press, 1988)

Faber and Faber for permission to reprint the following poems by Seamus Heaney: 'Follower' from *Death of a Naturalist* (1966); 'Bogland' from *Door into the Dark* (1969); 'The Tollund man' and 'The other side' from *Wintering Out* (1972); 'Mossbawn: two poems in dedication' and 'Exposure' from *North* (1975); 'The otter', 'A postcard from north Antrim' and 'The harvest bow' from *Field Work* (1979); 'Sloe gin' from *Station Island* (1984); 'Clearances' (extracts) and 'The haw lantern' from *The Haw Lantern* (1987); for permission to reprint the following poems by Louis MacNeice: 'Prayer before birth', 'Carrickfergus', 'Autobiography', 'Snow', 'Autumn journal' (extract), 'The sunlight on the garden',

325

'Meeting-point', 'The introduction', 'Elegy for minor poets', 'The truisms', 'The taxis' and 'Charon' from *Collected Poems* (1969); for permission to reprint the following poems by Paul Muldoon: 'The field hospital' from *New Weather* (1973); 'The mixed marriage' and 'Ma' from *Mules* (1977); 'Cuba', 'Anseo', 'The weepies' and 'Truce' from *Why Brownlee Left* (1980); 'Quoof', 'Gathering mushrooms' and 'Aisling' from *Quoof* (1983); 'Meeting the British' from *Meeting the British* (1987); for permission to reprint the following poems by Tom Paulin: 'Settlers', 'Under the eyes' and 'Cadaver politic' from *A State of Justice* (1977); 'Personal column', 'A lyric afterwards' and 'Surveillances' from *The Strange Museum* (1980); 'Desertmartin', 'The other voice' and 'Manichean geography I' from *Liberty Tree* (1983); 'An Ulster unionist walks the streets of London' from *Fivemiletown* (1987)

Farrar, Straus and Giroux for permission to reprint the following poems by Seamus Heaney: 'Follower' from *Death of a Naturalist* (1966); 'Bogland' from *Door into the Dark* (1969); 'The Tollund man' and 'The other side' from *Wintering Out* (1972); 'Mossbawn: two poems in dedication' and 'Exposure' from *North* (1975); 'The otter', 'A postcard from north Antrim' and 'The harvest bow' from *Field Work* (1979); 'Sloe gin' from *Station Island* (1984); 'Clearances' (extracts) and 'The haw lantern' from *The Haw Lantern* (1987)

Padraic Fiacc for permission to reprint the following poems: 'Soldiers' from *Nights in the Bad Place* (Blackstaff Press, 1977); 'The British connection', 'Enemy encounter', 'Intimate letter 1973' and 'Saint Coleman's song for a flight' from *Missa Terribilis* (Blackstaff Press, 1986)

Michael Foley for permission to reprint the following poems: 'True life love stories' (extracts) and 'Lucky Eugene' from *True Life Love Stories* (Blackstaff Press, 1976); 'A provincial adolescence', 'Brothers and sisters', 'The middle manager in paradise' and 'On the waterfront' from *The GO Situation* (Blackstaff Press, 1982)

Gallery Press for permission to reprint the following poems by Ciaran Carson: 'Belfast confetti', 'Campaign', 'Dresden', 'The Irish for no' and 'Asylum' from *The Irish for No* (1987); 'The mouth', 'The knee' and 'Hamlet' from *Belfast Confetti* (1989); for permission to reprint the following poems by Gerald Dawe: 'A question of convenants', 'Seamen's Mission' and 'Solstice' from *The Lundys Letter* (1985); 'The likelihood of snow/The danger of fire' from *Sunday School* (1990); for permission to reprint the following poems by Seamus Deane: 'Return', 'Roots', 'Fording the river', 'The brethren', 'A burial' and 'History lessons' from *Selected Poems* (1989); for permission to reprint the following poems by John Hughes: 'Dog day lesson', 'Knowingness' and 'A respect for law and order' from *The Something in Particular* (1986); for permission to reprint the following poem by Derek Mahon: 'Achill' from *Antarctica* (1985); for permission to reprint the following poems by John Montague: 'Hearth song' from *Mount Eagle* (1988); 'Like dolmens round my childhood, the old people', 'The trout', 'All legendary obstacles', 'The cage', 'The same gesture', 'Last journey', 'Herbert Street revisited' and 'The silver flask' from *New Selected Poems* (1989); for permission to reprint the following poems by Frank Ormsby: 'Winter offerings', 'A day in August' and 'Spot the ball' from *A Store of Candles* (1977); 'The war photographers', 'A northern spring' (extracts) and 'Home' from *A Northern Spring* (1986); for permission to reprint the following poems by James Simmons: 'The influence of natural objects', 'Stephano remembers', 'Lullaby for Rachael', 'Join me in celebrating', 'A birthday poem', 'One of the boys', 'Didn't he ramble', 'Eden', 'After Eden', 'For Imelda', 'The honeymoon' and 'From the Irish' from *Selected Poems 1956-86* (1986)

Goldsmith Press for permission to reprint the following poems by Padraic Fiacc: 'Gloss' and 'First Movement' from *Odour of Blood* (1973)

The estate of John Hewitt for permission to reprint the following poems: 'I write for . . .' from *Scissors for a One-armed Tailor* (privately published); 'Once alien here', 'An Irishman in Coventry', 'O country people', 'Because I paced my thought' and 'The ram's horn' from *Collected Poems 1932–1967* (MacGibbon and Kee, 1968); 'The scar', 'From the Tibetan' and 'The search' from *Out of my Time* (Blackstaff Press, 1974); 'Substance and shadow' and 'A local poet' from *Time Enough* (Blackstaff Press, 1976); 'A father's death', and 'Sonnets for Roberta (1954)' (extracts) from *The Rain Dance* (Blackstaff Press, 1978)

Robert Johnstone for permission to reprint the following poems: 'New incidents in the life of Shelley' (extract) and 'Every cache' (extracts) from *Breakfast in a Bright Room* (Blackstaff Press, 1983); 'Robot camera', 'Undertakers', 'Eden says no' and 'The fruit of knowledge' from *Eden to Edenderry* (Blackstaff Press, 1989)

Michael Longley and Peters Fraser and Dunlop for permission to reprint the following poems: 'No continuing city', 'Swans mating', 'Caravan', 'In Memoriam', 'Wounds', 'Fleance', 'Man lying on a wall', 'The linen industry', 'Peace', 'The third light' and 'An Amish Rug' from *Poems 1963–1983* (Salamander Press, 1984/Penguin Books, 1985); 'Ghetto' from *Gorse Fires* (Secker and Warburg, forthcoming 1991)

Roy McFadden for permission to reprint the following poems: 'Epithalamium' and 'Letter to an Irish novelist' from *Flowers for a Lady* (Routledge, 1945); 'Memories of Chinatown' (extract) and 'Contemplations of Mary' from *The Garryowen* (Chatto and Windus, 1971);

'Stringer's field' from *Verifications* (Blackstaff Press, 1977); 'The Grand Central Hotel' from *The Selected Roy McFadden* (Blackstaff Press, 1983); 'My mother's young sister' and 'For the record' from *After Seymour's Funeral* (Blackstaff Press, 1990)

Medbh McGuckian for permission to reprint the following poem: 'The presence' from *Two Women, Two Shores* (New Poets Series Inc, Baltimore, Maryland, 1989)

Tom Matthews for permission to reprint the following poems: 'Private but sulphurous', 'Happy Arabia', 'Robert sat', 'Cowboy film' and 'Even the whales' from *Dr Wilson as an Arab* (Holysmoke Press, 1974)

John Montague for permission to reprint the following poems: 'A drink of milk' and 'A welcoming party' from *Poisoned Lands* (MacGibbon and Kee, 1961; revised edition, Dolmen Press, 1977); 'Windharp' from *A Slow Dance* (Dolmen Press, 1975)

Oxford University Press for permission to reprint the following poems by Medbh McGuckian: 'Tulips', 'Mr McGregor's garden', 'The sofa', 'The seed-picture', 'The flower master' and 'The flitting' from *The Flower Master* (1982); 'On not being your lover' and 'The sitting' from *Venus and the Rain* (1984); 'Little house, big house' from *On Ballycastle Beach* (1988); for permission to reprint the following poems by Derek Mahon: 'In Carrowdore churchyard', 'An unborn child', 'The spring vacation', 'Ecclesiastes', 'The snow party', 'The last of the fire kings', 'Poem beginning with a line by Cavafy', 'Bruce Ismay's soliloquy', 'A disused shed in Co. Wexford' and 'A refusal to mourn' from *Poems 1962–1978* (1979); 'Courtyards in Delft' from *The Hunt by Night* (1982)

Secker and Warburg for permission to reprint the following poems by William Peskett: 'The question of time', 'Star and sea', 'The inheritors', 'Bottles in the Zoological Museum' and 'Window dressing' from *The Night-owl's Dissection* (1975); 'From Belfast to Suffolk' from *Survivors* (1980); for permission to reprint the following poems by W.R. Rodgers: 'Stormy night', 'The net', 'Lent', 'The swan', and 'Resurrection: an Easter sequence' (extracts) from *Europa and the Bull* (1952)

Sidgwick and Jackson for permission to reprint the following poems by Patrick Williams: 'Lost seed', 'Trails', 'Rhapsody on Main Street', 'In the dark', 'Passing through' and 'A baby in the house' from *Trails* (1981)

Wake Forest University Press for permission to reprint the following poems by Ciaran Carson: 'Belfast confetti', 'Campaign', 'Dresden', 'The Irish for no' and 'Asylum' from *The Irish for No* (1987); 'The mouth', 'The knee' and 'Hamlet' from *Belfast Confetti* (1989); for permission to reprint the following poems by John Montague: 'Hearth song' from *Mount Eagle* (1988); 'Like dolmens round my childhood, the old people', 'The trout', 'All legendary obstacles', 'The cage', 'The same gesture', 'Last journey', 'Herbert Street revisited' and 'The silver flask' from *New Selected Poems* (1989); for permission to reprint the following poems by Paul Muldoon: 'The field hospital' from *New Weather* (1973); 'The mixed marriage' and 'Ma' from *Mules* (1977); 'Cuba', 'Anseo', 'The weepies' and 'Truce' from *Why Brownlee Left* (1980); 'Quoof', 'Gathering mushrooms' and 'Aisling' from *Quoof* (1983); 'Meeting the British' from *Meeting the British* (1987)

The publishers have made every effort to trace and acknowledge copyright holders. We apologise for any omissions in the above list and we will welcome additions or amendments to it for inclusion in any reprint edition.

INDEX OF TITLES AND FIRST LINES

331

NOTE ON REVISIONS

A number of authors' revisions and amendments have been incorporated in this second edition. Roy McFadden, whose poems 'Bigamy' (*from* 'Memories of Chinatown') and 'First letter to an Irish novelist' were revised for the first edition, has made further alterations to both poems; he has also rewritten parts of 'The Grand Central Hotel' and amended two lines in 'Contemplations of Mary'.

The selection of Derek Mahon's poems incorporates revisions made by Mahon for his volume, *Poems 1962–1978* (1979); the selection of John Montague's poems incorporates revisions made by Montague for his volume, *Selected Poems* (1982).